THE STUDENTS' JB

THE GOSPEL
ACCORDING TO SAINT LUKE

THE STUDENTS' J.B.

THE GOSPEL ACCORDING TO SAINT LUKE

With notes & commentary
by
K. S. L. Clark,
B.A.Oxon.

LONDON
DARTON, LONGMAN & TODD

First published in Great Britain in 1972 by
Darton, Longman & Todd Limited
89 Lillie Road, London SW6 1UD

Jerusalem Bible text and notes © 1966, 1967 and 1968
by Darton, Longman & Todd Ltd
and Doubleday & Company Inc.
Students' notes and commentary © 1972 by K S L Clark

Printed and bound in Great Britain by
Anchor Brendon Ltd, Tiptree, Essex

ISBN 0 232 51170 5

Reprinted 1975, 1978, 1980 and 1984

INTRODUCTION

By the time Luke wrote his gospel, possibly about A.D. 85, Christians were used to persecution. On the one hand were the Jews who hated them as a splinter group which broke the Law of Moses and spread false teaching; on the other were the Roman officials who suspected their political disloyalty, believing that they claimed there was another Emperor, Jesus (Acts 17:7). Luke therefore had a twofold purpose in writing. He wanted to show that Christianity had taken the place of Judaism in the purposes of God because Jesus was the fulfilment of Old Testament prophecy and Jewish history. He also wanted to make clear that Christ's is a spiritual kingdom, and no rival to imperial or kingly power. He produced his work in two parts, the gospel which tells the story from the birth of Jesus to the ascension, and the Acts of the Apostles which describes the expansion of the Church to Rome. Each book begins with a prologue which makes the connection clear.

Luke set his subject clearly in the period to which it belongs by mentioning contemporary rulers, and particularly in Acts which in some parts describes what he had himself experienced, he has been proved a careful and accurate writer. Roman writers in the second half of the first century have left evidence which is useful because it is non-Christian. Tacitus (c. 58–116), Suetonius (c. 75–140), and the younger Pliny (c. 61–114) hated and despised the Christians, the former describing Christianity as a deadly superstition which got its name from

Christus who 'suffered the extreme penalty during the reign of Tiberius at the hands of one of our procurators, Pontius Pilate' (*New Eusebius*, p. 2). Josephus, a Jewish historian who lived in Rome, is also important though he never mentioned Jesus, no doubt because he disapproved of Messiahs, nationalist leaders who came to the fore from time to time.

POLITICAL AND RELIGIOUS BACKGROUND TO THE NEW TESTAMENT

A. *The Roman Empire*

The Roman Republic collapsed in the struggle for power between Julius Caesar and Pompey, Octavian and Mark Antony. Murder, civil war, and dramatic suicide preceded the establishment of the Empire in 30 B.C. by Augustus, the title by which Octavian, great nephew of Caesar, is always known. His reign introduced a period of peace which lasted nearly a century. On his death in A.D. 14 he was succeeded by Tiberius who was Emperor at the time of the crucifixion, and died in 37. These two were cold and cruel but they were good administrators. Luke as an old man in the last quarter of the century, would remember bad successors chosen by the soldiers, particularly Nero who caused hundreds of Christians, including St Peter and St Paul, to be put to death in Rome in 64. Nero was followed by two able generals, Vespasian and then Titus. The idea of empire was inevitably associated with brute force and the winning of popular favour by any means that seemed to promise success. Luke showed the values of Jesus, and the kingdom of God, as being totally opposed to the objects and methods of the world.

B. *Palestine*

Palestine was conquered by the Romans under Pompey in 63 B.C. because it linked Syria and Egypt, already dependencies of Rome, and was necessary as a bulwark against Parthia, a rival empire in the east. By the time Jesus was born it had been put under the control of Herod the Great, a client king subordinate to Rome. He was not of royal blood and by race he was an Arab from Idumea in the south, but he had great political flair and backed the winning side in the struggle which preceded the reign of Augustus. He was very rich and to make himself popular with the Jews began to rebuild the Temple at Jerusalem on the most lavish scale. Violent and jealous in temperament, he ordered the execution of close members of his family, and St Matthew's story of the massacre of the infants at Bethlehem (Mt 2:16) is in keeping with what is known of him from other sources. On his death two years later his kingdom was divided amongst his sons. Archelaus, the eldest, was made king of Judaea but he was so tyrannical that a deputation of Jews went to Rome to demand his removal. He was deposed and Roman Governors were thenceforth responsible for Judaea, Pontius Pilate (26–36) being one of a series. Another son, Herod Antipas, was made ruler of Galilee, while Philip the third son had Ituraea, Gaulanitis, and Trachonitis in the north. The Herod of this gospel is Herod Antipas.

The government continued on these lines until the Jews could no longer endure Roman control and revolted. The Jewish War lasted from 66–70. After fierce fighting and a prolonged siege of Jerusalem, the Jews were defeated by the Roman army under Titus. The city was laid waste, the Temple was destroyed, and a large proportion of the population fled the country. It was the beginning of centuries of exile and the end of Jewish nationalist hopes until after World War I: General Dayan won Jerusalem for the new Jewish state of Israel in 1967. The gospels record Jesus as predicting the terrible tragedy which would befall Jerusalem and the people.

Jewish affairs under the Roman government

Because the Jews were difficult to control, strictly Jewish matters were dealt with by the Sanhedrin, the Jewish Council under the presidency of the high priest. It was this body which had Jesus arrested, and in it were represented two strongly opposed factions amongst the people:

(1) *The Sadducees* These were families claiming descent from Zadok, High Priest in King David's time: they formed the wealthy aristocracy from which the priests were drawn. As priests they functioned only in the Temple because sacrifice might be offered nowhere else. They kept to the literal meaning of the scriptures, and believed neither in the resurrection of the dead nor in angels. They did not expect a Messiah, a deliverer of the people sent by God, and were friendly with the Romans.

(2) *The Pharisees* These were highly educated laymen who held not only to the Law of Moses to be found in the Scriptures, but to the interpretations of the Law which had grown up over the years, called the Oral Law or the Traditions. It was the Oral Law which laid down the rules for the ritual washing before meals, for the activities forbidden on the sabbath, for fasting, and for the right behaviour in the varied aspects of family life. Pharisees regarded people born outside the Law,

8

heathen or gentiles as non-Jews were called, as unclean; and they would have nothing to do with lax Jews who mixed with gentiles freely and failed to perform ceremonies of purification afterwards, the tax-gatherers and sinners of the gospels. Pharisees believed in the resurrection of the dead, and expected the Messiah. The synagogues (meeting houses) were the particular sphere of their influence, and there the people gathered every sabbath to hear the Scriptures read and explained, and to pray. The one Temple was in Jerusalem, but there were synagogues in the villages and towns elsewhere.

(3) *The Scribes* These were specialists in the Scriptures, the men who through their interpretations had brought the Oral Law into being. They always based their teaching on what learned predecessors had said, and objected to Jesus so strongly because he taught on his own authority. Most of the scribes were Pharisees.

C. *Language and religion within the Empire*

Greek colonisation had been taking place in the Middle East long before the conquests of Alexander the Great in the fourth century B.C. accelerated the process. As a result of this there was a fusion of Greek religion and culture with those of the east, and the emergence of a distinctive culture known as Hellenism, Greek being the predominant element, and Greek becoming the common language spoken everywhere. Many people were bilingual, speaking the particular language of their birthplace as well as Greek. In Palestine for instance, the local language was Aramaic (Hebrew was only used for religious services), and it was Aramaic that was spoken by Jesus and his disciples. After the resurrection, however, when the apostles in due course preached the Gospel outside Palestine, they naturally used Greek.

That is why the documents which were eventually collected to form the New Testament, were originally written in Greek.

A great variety of gods were worshipped in the Hellenistic world, Mesopotamian and Egyptian as well as Greek and Roman. They made no demands on conduct and none claimed universal authority though all promised salvation from the pain and danger of existence, and the evil influence of the stars. Intellectuals despised the worship of the gods as being too crude, and preferred to guide their lives by some system of philosophy. But everyone was superstitious, and astrologers, fortune tellers, and magicians flourished. Against this background the Jews played an extraordinary and creative role. For three centuries or more before Christ, they had been leaving their homeland to make their fortunes abroad, and by the time of Augustus there were communities of Jews in probably all the cities of note in the eastern part of the Empire. They are known as Jews of the Dispersion. Each community was centred on its synagogue, and though its members spoke Greek and dressed like their heathen neighbours, they had as little to do with them as possible. The Hebrew Scriptures had by this time been translated into Greek, the version known as the Septuagint or LXX for short, and they held fast to their Law. Their high moral standards and disciplined way of life attracted some of the heathen who began to inquire into the Jewish belief in the One God, Creator, Almighty. Converts were made, and after preparation if they were ready to give up their pagan habits, they were allowed to join in synagogue worship. They were called God-fearers and remained on the fringe, not being allowed to join in the presentations of offerings in the Temple at Jerusalem, should they go there. Others, ready to go further and accept circumcision as the sign of the special relationship between God and His people, were admitted to full membership of the religion and were called proselytes. It was amongst the God-fearers and proselytes that the apostles made many converts to Christianity when they began to preach outside Palestine, and there is no doubt that Luke came from such a background.

D. *The Author*

The earliest writing that states that Luke was the author of the third gospel can be dated about 185, but the statement is based on a tradition that goes much further back. He was said to be Luke the doctor, mentioned by St Paul in his letter to the Colossians (Colossians 4:16) and also in Philemon 24. Some parts of Acts are written in the first person plural, suggesting that the author accompanied St Paul on some of his missionary journeys. The style and vocabulary are those of an educated Greek, and he was obviously well acquainted with the Greek version of the Scriptures, the Septuagint.

E. *The Gospels*

The gospels are a unique form of literature. The word means 'good news' so the basic idea is that they bring a message. The message is that God has provided salvation from sin, fear, and death for all mankind through His Son, Jesus Christ. Jesus, God Incarnate (God made flesh) demonstrated what human life should be like: he also gave direct instruction about the right values to pursue, teaching that God is our heavenly Father who cares for each one of us. Then his death and resurrection not only show us that pain and death can be the gateway to fuller life but are the means whereby we may attain it because they were preliminary to his ascension and the outpouring of the Holy Spirit. The Holy Spirit was sent to dwell within the disciples and to guide them. Jesus was no longer visible to his disciples after the ascension but was with them wherever they happened to be. 'I am with you always; yes, to the end of time' (Mt 28:20).

In the early years after the resurrection the Gospel was transmitted by word of mouth. The Jews were used to being taught that way and so had accurate and retentive memories. It is thought that the stories of what Jesus did and said very soon fell into a generally accepted pattern, the story of his death and resurrection being the first to do so. There was delay before anything was written down because the first Christians confidently expected our Lord to return in glory from heaven and establish the kingdom of God. As this hope began to fade and the leaders of the Church grew old, the Gospel was committed to writing.

There is a second-century tradition that the first gospel was written by Matthew, the tax collector, in Aramaic for the Palestinian Christians converted from Judaism, but it is St Mark's which has the most primitive characteristics and which very many modern scholars believe to be the earliest. According to tradition St Peter in Rome made Mark write down what he himself was accustomed to teach, and as Peter was martyred during the persecutions of Nero's reign about 64, St Mark's gospel must have been completed before that date.

St Matthew and St Luke include the whole, or nearly the whole of St Mark as well as material unknown to one another. They are not thought to have known each other's work though they both drew on a common say-

12

ings source known as 'Q' from the German 'quelle' meaning 'source' (i.e. the unknown source), and they may well have been contemporary, producing their work possibly in the eighties.

These three gospels, Mt, Mk, and Lk are known as the synoptic gospels because they tell the story in much the same way. (Synoptic = seen from the same point of view.) They were of course written in Greek though in Mk a few words and phrases of the original Aramaic appear in quotations of spoken words.

St John's gospel was the last to be written, the author according to tradition being John Zebedee (Lk 5:10), and there are good grounds for thinking that it was in circulation before the end of the first century. There is a connection between Lk and Jn and they may have had access to a common source.

Note
Interpretation of the text
The following works have been consulted:
    Peake's Commentary: Luke by G. W. H. Lampe
    The Gospel according to St Luke by A. R. C. Leaney
    The Gospel according to St Luke by J. M. Creed
    The Sayings of Jesus by T. W. Manson
    The Jerusalem Bible, Standard Edition

THE GOSPEL
ACCORDING TO SAINT LUKE

Note. In this Gospel, the text is printed in paragraphs, and not as a succession of separate units called verses. In case any comparison with other versions is necessary, the verse-numbers (as used in the Vulgate, Authorised Version, etc.) are printed in the margin and a dot (·) shows where the numbered verse begins, if this is in the middle of a line. (If a verse number is missing, this is because the Jerusalem Bible follows a text that differs from that followed by the older translations.)

Italic type indicates an identifiable quotation, normally from a book of the Old Testament.

Prologue

1 **1** Seeing that many others have undertaken to draw up accounts of the events that have taken place
2 among us, ·exactly as these were handed down to us by those who from the outset were eyewitnesses and
3 ministers of the word, ·I in my turn, after carefully going over the whole story from the beginning, have decided
4 to write an ordered account for you, Theophilus, ·so that your Excellency may learn how well founded the teaching is that you have received.

I. THE BIRTH AND HIDDEN LIFE OF JOHN THE BAPTIST AND OF JESUS

The birth of John the Baptist foretold

5 In the days of King Herod of Judaea there lived a priest called Zechariah who belonged to the Abijah section of the priesthood, and he had a wife, Elizabeth
6 by name, who was a descendant of Aaron. ·Both were worthy in the sight of God, and scrupulously observed all the commandments and observances of the Lord.
7 But they were childless: Elizabeth was barren and they were both getting on in years.
8 Now it was the turn of Zechariah's section[a] to serve, and he was exercising his priestly office before God

1 a. The 24 families of the 'sons of Aaron' were responsible in rotation for service in the Temple, and in each class or family the individual was chosen by lot. See 1 Ch 24.

17

when it fell to him by lot, as the ritual custom was, to 9
enter the Lord's sanctuary and burn incense there.[b]
And at the hour of incense the whole congregation 10
was outside, praying.

Then there appeared to him the angel of the Lord, 11
standing on the right of the altar of incense. ·The sight 12
disturbed Zechariah and he was overcome with fear.
But the angel said to him, 'Zechariah, do not be afraid, 13
your prayer has been heard. Your wife Elizabeth is to
bear you a son and you must name him John.[c] ·He will 14
be your joy and delight and many will rejoice at his
birth, ·for he will be great in the sight of the Lord; he 15
must drink no wine, no strong drink.[d] Even from his
mother's womb he will be filled with the Holy Spirit,
and he will bring back many of the sons of Israel to the 16
Lord their God. ·With the spirit and power of Elijah, he 17
will go before him *to turn the hearts of fathers towards their
children*[e] and the disobedient back to the wisdom that
the virtuous have, preparing for the Lord a people fit
for him.' ·Zechariah said to the angel, '*How can I be sure* 18
of this?[f] I am an old man and my wife is getting on
in years.' ·The angel replied, 'I am Gabriel who stand in 19
God's presence, and I have been sent to speak to you
and bring you this good news. ·Listen! Since you have 20
not believed my words, which will come true at their
appointed time, you will be silenced and have no power
of speech until this has happened.' ·Meanwhile the 21
people were waiting for Zechariah and were surprised
that he stayed in the sanctuary so long. ·When he came 22
out he could not speak to them, and they realised that
he had received a vision in the sanctuary. But he could
only make signs to them, and remained dumb.

When his time of service came to an end he returned 23
home. ·Some time later his wife Elizabeth conceived, 24

25 and for five months she kept to herself. ·'The Lord has done this for me' she said 'now that it has pleased him to take away the humiliation I suffered among men.'

The annunciation

26 In the sixth month the angel Gabriel was sent by
27 God to a town in Galilee called Nazareth, ·to a virgin betrothed to a man named Joseph, of the House of
28 David; and the virgin's name was Mary. ·He went in and said to her, 'Rejoice, so highly favoured! The Lord is
29 with you.' ·She was deeply disturbed by these words and
30 asked herself what this greeting could mean, ·but the angel said to her, 'Mary, do not be afraid; you have
31 won God's favour. ·Listen! You are to conceive and
32 bear a son, and you must name him Jesus. ·He will be great and will be called Son of the Most High. The Lord
33 God will give him the throne of his ancestor David; ·he will rule over the House of Jacob for ever and his reign
34 will have no end.' ·Mary said to the angel, 'But how
35 can this come about, since I am a virgin?'*g* ·'The Holy Spirit will come upon you' the angel answered 'and the power of the Most High will cover you with its shadow. And so the child will be holy and will be called Son of
36 God. ·Know this too: your kinswoman Elizabeth has, in her old age, herself conceived a son, and she whom
37 people called barren is now in her sixth month, ·*for*

b. The priest tended the brazier on the altar of incense in front of the Most Holy Place.

c. The meaning of the name is 'Yahweh is gracious'.

d. See Nb 6:1, where this abstinence is required in anyone performing a vow to the Lord.

e. Ml 3:23–24

f. Zechariah asks for a sign in a way reminiscent of Abram, Gn 15:8.

g. Lit. 'since I do not know man'.

nothing is impossible to God.'ʰ ·'I am the handmaid of 38
the Lord,' said Mary 'let what you have said be done to
me.' And the angel left her.

The visitation

Mary set out at that time and went as quickly as she 39
could to a town in the hill country of Judah. ·She went 40
into Zechariah's house and greeted Elizabeth. ·Now as 41
soon as Elizabeth heard Mary's greeting, the child leapt
in her womb and Elizabeth was filled with the Holy Spirit.
She gave a loud cry and said, 'Of all women you are the 42
most blessed, and blessed is the fruit of your womb.
Why should I be honoured with a visit from the mother 43
of my Lord? ·For the moment your greeting reached 44
my ears, the child in my womb leapt for joy. ·Yes, 45
blessed is she who believed that the promise made her
by the Lord would be fulfilled.'

The Magnificat

And Mary*ⁱ* said: 46

'My soul proclaims the greatness of the Lord
and my spirit *exults in God my saviour;* 47
because *he has looked upon his lowly handmaid.* 48
Yes, from this day forward all generations will call
me blessed,
for the Almighty has done great things for me. 49
Holy is his name,
and *his mercy reaches from age to age for those who* 50
fear him.
He has shown the power of his arm, 51
he has routed the proud of heart.
He has pulled down princes from their thrones *and* 52
exalted the lowly.

20

53　　*The hungry he has filled with good things,* the rich
　　　　sent empty away.

54　　*He has come to the help of Israel his servant, mindful*
　　　　of his mercy

55　　—according to the promise he made to our
　　　　ancestors—
　　　　of his mercy to Abraham and to his descendants for
　　　　ever.'

56　　Mary stayed with Elizabeth about three months and
　　then went back home.

The birth of John the Baptist and visit of the neighbours

57　　Meanwhile the time came for Elizabeth to have her
58　child, and she gave birth to a son; ·and when her
　　neighbours and relations heard that the Lord had
　　shown her so great a kindness, they shared her joy.

The circumcision of John the Baptist

59　　Now on the eighth day they came to circumcise the
　　child; they were going to call[j] him Zechariah after his
60　father, ·but his mother spoke up. 'No,' she said 'he is to
61　be called John.' ·They said to her, 'But no one in your
62　family has that name', ·and made signs to his father to
63　find out what he wanted him called. ·The father asked
　　for a writing-tablet and wrote, 'His name is John'. And
64　they were all astonished. ·At that instant his power of
65　speech returned and he spoke and praised God. ·All
　　their neighbours were filled with awe and the whole affair
　　was talked about throughout the hill country of Judaea.

h. Gn 8:14.
i. Mary's canticle is reminiscent of Hannah's, 1 S 2: 1–10. Other
quotations and allusions in the Magnificat are: 1 S 1:11; Ps
103:17; Ps 111:9; Jb 5:11 and 12:19; Ps 98:3; Ps 107:9; Is 41:8–9.
j. The name was normally given at the time of circumcision.

All those who heard of it treasured it in their hearts. 66
'What will this child turn out to be?' they wondered.
And indeed the hand of the Lord was with him.

The Benedictus

His father Zechariah was filled with the Holy Spirit 67
   and spoke this prophecy:

'*Blessed be the Lord, the God of Israel,*[k] 68
for he has visited his people, he has come to
   their rescue
and he has raised up for us a power for 69
   salvation
in the House of his servant David,
even as he proclaimed, 70
by the mouth of his holy prophets from ancient
   times,
that he would save us from our enemies 71
and from the hands of all who hate us.
Thus he shows mercy to our ancestors, 72
thus *he remembers* his holy *covenant,*[l]
the oath he swore 73
to our father Abraham
that he would grant us, free from fear, 74
to be delivered from the hands of our enemies,
to serve him in holiness and virtue 75
in his presence, all our days.
And you, little child, 76
you shall be called Prophet of the Most High,
for you will go before the Lord
to prepare the way for him.
To give his people knowledge of salvation 77
through the forgiveness of their sins;
this by the tender mercy of our God 78

who from on high will bring the rising Sun to
visit us,
79 to give light to *those who live
in darkness and the shadow of death,*[m]
and to guide our feet
into the way of peace.'

The hidden life of John the Baptist

80 Meanwhile the child grew up and his spirit matured.
And he lived out in the wilderness until the day he
appeared openly to Israel.

The birth of Jesus and visit of the shepherds

1 2 Now at this time Caesar Augustus[a] issued a decree
2 for a census of the whole world to be taken. ·This
census—the first[b]—took place while Quirinius was
3 governor of Syria, ·and everyone went to his own town
4 to be registered. ·So Joseph set out from the town of
Nazareth in Galilee and travelled up to Judaea, to the
town of David called Bethlehem, since he was of David's
5 House and line, ·in order to be registered together with
6 Mary, his betrothed, who was with child. ·While they
7 were there the time came for her to have her child, ·and
she gave birth to a son, her first-born.[c] She wrapped him
in swaddling clothes, and laid him in a manger because
8 there was no room for them at the inn. ·In the countryside close by there were shepherds who lived in the
fields and took it in turns to watch their flocks during
9 the night. ·The angel of the Lord appeared to them and
the glory of the Lord shone round them. They were
10 terrified, ·but the angel said, 'Do not be afraid. Listen,

k. Ps 41:13.   **l.** Lv 26:42.   **m.** Is 9:1.
2 a. Emperor of Rome 30 B.C. to A.D. 14.   **b.** About 8–6 B.C.
c. The term does not necessarily imply younger brothers.

I bring you news of great joy, a joy to be shared by the whole people. ·Today in the town of David a saviour has 11 been born to you; he is Christ the Lord. ·And here is a 12 sign for you: you will find a baby wrapped in swaddling clothes and lying in a manger.' ·And suddenly with the 13 angel there was a great throng of the heavenly host, praising God and singing:

> 'Glory to God in the highest heaven,' 14
> and peace to men who enjoy his favour'.

Now when the angels had gone from them into 15 heaven, the shepherds said to one another, 'Let us go to Bethlehem and see this thing that has happened which the Lord has made known to us'. ·So they hurried away 16 and found Mary and Joseph, and the baby lying in the manger. ·When they saw the child they repeated what 17 they had been told about him, ·and everyone who heard 18 it was astonished at what the shepherds had to say. ·As 19 for Mary, she treasured all these things and pondered them in her heart. ·And the shepherds went back 20 glorifying and praising God for all they had heard and seen; it was exactly as they had been told.

The circumcision of Jesus

When the eighth day came and the child was to be 21 circumcised, they gave him the name Jesus, the name the angel had given him before his conception.

Jesus is presented in the Temple

And when the day came for them to be purified[d] as 22 laid down by the Law of Moses, they took him up to Jerusalem to present him to the Lord—·observing what 23 stands written in the Law of the Lord: *Every first-born male must be consecrated to the Lord*[e]—·and also to offer 24

24

in sacrifice, in accordance with what is said in the Law of
the Lord, *a pair of turtledoves or two young pigeons.*[f]
25 Now in Jerusalem there was a man named Simeon. He
was an upright and devout man; he looked forward to
Israel's comforting and the Holy Spirit rested on him.
26 It had been revealed to him by the Holy Spirit that he
would not see death until he had set eyes on the Christ
27 of the Lord.[g] •Prompted by the Spirit he came to the
Temple; and when the parents brought in the child
28 Jesus to do for him what the Law required, •he took
him into his arms and blessed God; and he said:

The Nunc Dimittis

29   'Now, Master, you can let your servant go in
         peace,
30   just as you promised;
         because my eyes have seen the salvation
31   which you have prepared for all the nations to
         see,
32   a light to enlighten the pagans
         and the glory of your people Israel'.

The Prophecy of Simeon

33   As the child's father and mother stood there won-
dering at the·things that were being said about him,
34 Simeon blessed them and said to Mary his mother,
'You see this child: he is destined for the fall and for
the rising of many in Israel, destined to be a sign that is
35 rejected—·and a sword will pierce your own soul too—
so that the secret thoughts of many may be laid bare'.

d. The mother needed to be 'purified'; the child had to be
'redeemed'.
e. Ex 13:2.   **f.** The offering of the poor, Lv 5:7.
g. 'The anointed one of God'.

The prophecy of Anna

There was a prophetess also, Anna the daughter of 36
Phanuel, of the tribe of Asher. She was well on in years.
Her days of girlhood over, she had been married for
seven years ·before becoming a widow. She was now 37
eighty-four years old and never left the Temple, serving
God night and day with fasting and prayer. ·She came 38
by just at that moment and began to praise God; and
she spoke of the child to all who looked forward to the
deliverance of Jerusalem.[h]

The hidden life of Jesus at Nazareth

When they had done everything the Law of the Lord 39
required, they went back to Galilee, to their own town
of Nazareth. ·Meanwhile the child grew to maturity, 40
and he was filled with wisdom; and God's favour was
with him.

Jesus among the doctors of the Law

Every year his parents used to go to Jerusalem for the 41
feast of the Passover. ·When he was twelve years old, 42
they went up for the feast as usual. ·When they were on 43
their way home after the feast, the boy Jesus stayed
behind in Jerusalem without his parents knowing it.
They assumed he was with the caravan, and it was only 44
after a day's journey that they went to look for him
among their relations and acquaintances. ·When they 45
failed to find him they went back to Jerusalem looking
for him everywhere.

Three days later, they found him in the Temple, 46
sitting among the doctors, listening to them, and asking
them questions; ·and all those who heard him were 47
astounded at his intelligence and his replies. ·They were 48

overcome when they saw him, and his mother said to him, 'My child, why have you done this to us? See how worried your father and I have been, looking for you.'
49 'Why were you looking for me?' he replied 'Did you not know that I must be busy with my Father's affairs?'
50 But they did not understand what he meant.

The hidden life at Nazareth resumed

51 He then went down with them and came to Nazareth and lived under their authority. His mother stored up all
52 these things in her heart. ·And Jesus increased in wisdom, in stature, and in favour with God and men.

II. PRELUDE TO THE PUBLIC MINISTRY OF JESUS

The preaching of John the Baptist

1 **3** In the fifteenth year of Tiberius Caesar's reign,[a] when Pontius Pilate[b] was governor of Judaea, Herod[c] tetrarch of Galilee, his brother Philip[d] tetrarch of the lands of Ituraea and Trachonitis, Lysanias tetrarch of
2 Abilene, ·during the pontificate of Annas and Caiaphas,[e] the word of God came to John son of Zechariah, in the

h. I.e. Israel. Jerusalem is the holy city.
3 a. By Roman dating, the 15th year of Tiberius Caesar's reign was August A.D. 28 to August A.D. 29; by the Syrian method, it was Sept.–Oct. A.D. 27 to Sept.–Oct. A.D. 28. At that time, Jesus was between 33 and 36 years old. The mistake in calculating 'the Christian era' results from taking Lk 3:23 as an exact statement.
b. Procurator of Judaea A.D. 26–36.
c. Herod Antipas, tetrarch of Galilee and Peraea 4 B.C. to A.D. 39.
d. Tetrarch from 4 B.C. to A.D. 34.
e. Caiaphas was high priest from A.D. 18 to 36. His father-in-law, Annas, is associated with him here and elsewhere; he had been high priest earlier and presumably still had great influence.

wilderness. ·He went through the whole Jordan district 3
proclaiming a baptism of repentance for the forgiveness
of sins, ·as it is written in the book of the sayings of the 4
prophet Isaiah:

> *A voice cries in the wilderness:*
> *prepare a way for the Lord,*
> *make his paths straight.*
> *Every valley will be filled in,* 5
> *every mountain and hill be laid low,*
> *winding ways will be straightened*
> *and rough roads made smooth.*
> *And all mankind shall see the salvation of God.*ʄ 6

He said, therefore, to the crowds who came to be 7
baptised by him, 'Brood of vipers, who warned you to
fly from the retribution that is coming? ·But if you are 8
repentant, produce the appropriate fruits, and do not
think of telling yourselves, "We have Abraham for our
father" because, I tell you, God can raise children for
Abraham from these stones. ·Yes, even now the axe 9
is laid to the roots of the trees, so that any tree which
fails to produce good fruit will be cut down and thrown
on the fire.'

When all the people asked him, 'What must we do, 10
then?' ·he answered, 'If anyone has two tunics he must 11
share with the man who has none, and the one with
something to eat must do the same'. ·There were tax 12
collectors too who came for baptism, and these said to
him, 'Master, what must we do?' ·He said to them, 13
'Exact no more than your rate'. ·Some soldiers asked 14
him in their turn. 'What about us? What must we do?'
He said to them, 'No intimidation! No extortion! Be
content with your pay!'

A feeling of expectancy had grown among the people, 15

who were beginning to think that John might be the
16 Christ, ·so John declared before them all, 'I baptise you with water, but someone is coming, someone who is more powerful than I am, and I am not fit to undo the strap of his sandals; he will baptise you with the Holy
17 Spirit and fire. ·His winnowing-fan is in his hand to clear his threshing-floor and to gather the wheat into his barn; but the chaff he will burn in a fire that will never go out.'
18 As well as this, there were many other things he said to exhort the people and to announce the Good News to them.

John the Baptist imprisoned

19 But Herod the tetrarch, whom he criticised for his relations with his brother's wife Herodias and for all
20 the other crimes Herod had committed, ·added a further crime to all the rest by shutting John up in prison.

Jesus is baptised

21 Now when all the people had been baptised and while Jesus after his own baptism was at prayer, heaven
22 opened ·and the Holy Spirit descended on· him in bodily shape, like a dove. And a voice came from heaven, 'You are my Son, the Beloved; my favour rests on you'.

The ancestry of Jesus

23 When he started to teach, Jesus was about thirty years old, being the son, as it was thought, of Joseph
24 son of Heli, ·son of Matthat, son of Levi, son of Melchi,
25 son of Jannai, son of Joseph, ·son of Mattathias, son of
26 Amos, son of Nahum, son of Esli, son of Naggai, ·son of Maath, son of Mattathias, son of Semein, son of
27 Josech, son of Joda, ·son of Joanan, son of Rhesa, son of
f. Is 40:3–5.

29

Zerubbabel, son of Shealtiel, son of Neri, ·son of Melchi, 28
son of Addi, son of Cosam, son of Elmadam, son of Er,
·son of Joshua, son of Eliezer, son of Jorim, son of 29
Matthat, son of Levi, ·son of Symeon, son of Judah, 30
son of Joseph, son of Jonam, son of Eliakim, ·son of 31
Melea, son of Menna, son of Mattatha, son of Nathan,
son of David, ·son of Jesse, son of Obed, son of 32
Boaz, son of Sala, son of Nahshon, ·son of Amminadab, 33
son of Admin, son of Arni, son of Hezron, son of Perez,
son of Judah, ·son of Jacob, son of Isaac, son of Abraham, 34
son of Terah, son of Nahor, ·son of Serug, son of Reu, 35
son of Peleg, son of Eber, son of Shelah, ·son of Cainan, 36
son of Arphaxad, son of Shem, son of Noah, son of
Lamech, ·son of Methuselah, son of Enoch, son of Jared, 37
son of Mahalaleel, son of Cainan, ·son of Enos, son of 38
Seth, son of Adam, son of God.

Temptation in the wilderness

4 Filled with the Holy Spirit, Jesus left the Jordan 1
and was led by the Spirit through the wilderness,
being tempted there by the devil for forty days. During 2
that time he ate nothing and at the end he was hungry.
Then the devil said to him, 'If you are the Son of God, 3
tell this stone to turn into a loaf'. ·But Jesus replied, 4
'Scripture says: *Man does not live on bread alone*'.*a*

Then leading him to a height, the devil showed him in 5
a moment of time all the kingdoms of the world ·and 6
said to him, 'I will give you all this power and the glory
of these kingdoms, for it has been committed to me and
I give it to anyone I choose. ·Worship me, then, and it 7
shall all be yours.' ·But Jesus answered him, 'Scripture 8
says:

> *You must worship the Lord your God,*
> *and serve him alone*'.*b*

9   Then he led him to Jerusalem and made him stand on the parapet of the Temple. 'If you are the Son of God,'
10 he said to him 'throw yourself down from here, ·for scripture says:

> *He will put his angels in charge of you*
> *to guard you,*

and again:

11   *They will hold you up on their hands*
> *in case you hurt your foot against a stone'.*[c]

12 But Jesus answered him, 'It has been said:
> *You must not put the Lord your God to the test'.*[d]

13 Having exhausted all these ways of tempting him, the devil left him, to return at the appointed time.

III. THE GALILEAN MINISTRY

Jesus begins to preach

14   Jesus, with the power of the Spirit in him, returned to Galilee; and his reputation spread throughout the
15 countryside. ·He taught in their synagogues and everyone praised him.

Jesus at Nazareth

16   He came to Nazara, where he had been brought up, and went into the synagogue on the sabbath day as he
17 usually did. He stood up to read,[e] ·and they handed him the scroll of the prophet Isaiah. Unrolling the scroll he found the place where it is written:

18   *The spirit of the Lord has been given to me,*
> *for he has anointed me.*

4 a. Dt 8:3.   **b.** Dt 6:13.   **c.** Ps 91:11–12.   **d.** Dt 6:16.
e. Any adult man could be permitted by the president to read the scriptures.

He has sent me to bring the good news to the poor,
to proclaim liberty to captives
and to the blind new sight,
to set the downtrodden free,
to proclaim the Lord's year of favour[f]   19

He then rolled up the scroll, gave it back to the assistant 20
and sat down. And all eyes in the synagogue were fixed
on him. ·Then he began to speak to them, 'This text is 21
being fulfilled today even as you listen'. ·And he won 22
the approval of all, and they were astonished by the
gracious words that came from his lips.

They said, 'This is Joseph's son, surely?' ·But he 23
replied, 'No doubt you will quote me the saying,
"Physician, heal yourself" and tell me, "We have heard
all that happened in Capernaum, do the same here in
your own countryside" '. ·And he went on, 'I tell you 24
solemnly, no prophet is ever accepted in his own
country.

'There were many widows in Israel, I can assure you, 25
in Elijah's day, when heaven remained shut for three
years and six months and a great famine raged throughout the land, ·but Elijah was not sent to any one of these: 26
he was sent *to a widow at Zarephath, a Sidonian town.*[g]
And in the prophet Elisha's time there were many lepers 27
in Israel, but none of these was cured, except the Syrian
Naaman.'

When they heard this everyone in the synagogue was 28
enraged. ·They sprang to their feet and hustled him out 29
of the town; and they took him up to the brow of the
hill their town was built on, intending to throw him
down the cliff, ·but he slipped through the crowd and 30
walked away.

Jesus teaches in Capernaum and cures a demoniac

31 He went down to Capernaum, a town in Galilee,
32 and taught them on the sabbath. ·And his teaching made
a deep impression on them because he spoke with
authority.

33 In the synagogue there was a man who was possessed
by the spirit of an unclean devil, and it shouted at the
34 top of its voice, ·'Ha! What do you want with us, Jesus
of Nazareth? Have you come to destroy us? I know
35 who you are: the Holy One of God.' ·But Jesus said
sharply, 'Be quiet! Come out of him!' And the devil,
throwing the man down in front of everyone, went out
36 of him without hurting him at all. ·Astonishment seized
them and they were all saying to one another, 'What
teaching! He gives orders to unclean spirits with
37 authority and power and they come out.' ·And reports
of him went all through the surrounding countryside.

Cure of Simon's mother-in-law

38 Leaving the synagogue he went to Simon's house.
Now Simon's mother-in-law was suffering from a high
fever and they asked him to do something for her.
39 Leaning over her he rebuked the fever and it left her.
And she immediately got up and began to wait on them.

A number of cures

40 At sunset all those who had friends suffering from
diseases of one kind or another brought them to him,
41 and laying his hands on each he cured them. ·Devils
too came out of many people, howling, 'You are the
Son of God'. But he rebuked them and would not allow
them to speak because they knew that he was the Christ.

f. Is 61:1–2.   g. 1 K 17:9.

Jesus quietly leaves Capernaum and travels through Judaea

When daylight came he left the house and made his 42
way to a lonely place. The crowds went to look for him,
and when they had caught up with him they wanted to
prevent him leaving them, ·but he answered, 'I must 43
proclaim the Good News of the kingdom of God to the
other towns too, because that is what I was sent to do'.
And he continued his preaching in the synagogues of 44
Judaea.

The first four disciples are called

5 Now he was standing one day by the Lake of Gen- 1
nesaret, with the crowd pressing round him listening
to the word of God, ·when he caught sight of two boats 2
close to the bank. The fishermen had gone out of them
and were washing their nets. ·He got into one of the 3
boats—it was Simon's—and asked him to put out a little
from the shore. Then he sat down and taught the
crowds from the boat.

When he had finished speaking he said to Simon, 'Put 4
out into deep water and pay out your nets for a catch',
'Master,' Simon replied 'we worked hard all night long 5
and caught nothing, but if you say so, I will pay out the
nets.' ·And when they had done this they netted such a 6
huge number of fish that their nets began to tear, ·so 7
they signalled to their companions in the other boat to
come and help them; when these came, they filled the
two boats to sinking point.

When Simon Peter saw this he fell at the knees of 8
Jesus saying, 'Leave me, Lord; I am a sinful man'. ·For 9
he and all his companions were completely overcome
by the catch they had made; ·so also were James and 10
John, sons of Zebedee, who were Simon's partners. But

Jesus said to Simon, 'Do not be afraid; from now on it is
11 men you will catch'. ·Then, bringing their boats back to
land, they left everything and followed him.

Cure of a leper

12 Now Jesus was in one of the towns when a man
appeared, covered with leprosy. Seeing Jesus he fell on
his face and implored him. 'Sir,' he said 'if you want to,
13 you can cure me.' ·Jesus stretched out his hand, touched
him and said, 'Of course I want to! Be cured!' And the
14 leprosy left him at once. ·He ordered him to tell no one,
'But go and show yourself to the priest and make the
offering for your healing as Moses prescribed it, as
evidence for them'.

15 His reputation continued to grow, and large crowds
would gather to hear him and to have their sickness
16 cured, ·but he would always go off to some place where
he could be alone and pray.

Cure of a paralytic

17 Now he was teaching one day, and among the
audience there were Pharisees and doctors of the Law
who had come from every village in Galilee, from
Judaea and from Jerusalem. And the Power of the
18 Lord was behind his works of healing. ·Then some men
appeared, carying on a bed a paralysed man whom
they were trying to bring in and lay down in front of him.
19 But as the crowd made it impossible to find a way of
getting him in, they went up on to the flat roof and
lowered him and his stretcher down through the tiles
into the middle of the gathering, in front of Jesus.
20 Seeing their faith he said, 'My friend, your sins are
21 forgiven you'. ·The scribes and the Pharisees began to
think this over. 'Who is this man talking blasphemy?

35

Who can forgive sins but God alone?' ·But Jesus, aware 22
of their thoughts, made them this reply, 'What are these
thoughts you have in your hearts? ·Which of these is 23
easier: to say, "Your sins are forgiven you" or to say,
"Get up and walk"? ·But to prove to you that the Son 24
of Man has authority on earth to forgive sins,'—he said
to the paralysed man—'I order you: get up, and pick
up your stretcher and go home.' ·And immediately 25
before their very eyes he got up, picked up what he had
been lying on and went home praising God.

They were all astounded and praised God, and were 26
filled with awe, saying, 'We have seen strange things
today'.

The call of Levi

When he went out after this, he noticed a tax collector, 27
Levi by name, sitting by the customs house, and said to
him, 'Follow me'. ·And leaving everything he got up 28
and followed him.

Eating with sinners in Levi's house

In his honour Levi held a great reception in his house, 29
and with them at table was a large gathering of tax
collectors and others. ·The Pharisees and their scribes 30
complained to his disciples and said, 'Why do you eat
and drink with tax collectors and sinners?' ·Jesus said 31
to them in reply, 'It is not those who are well who need
the doctor, but the sick. ·I have not come to call the 32
virtuous, but sinners to repentance.'

Discussion on fasting

They then said to him, 'John's disciples are always 33
fasting and saying prayers, and the disciples of the
Pharisees too, but yours go on eating and drinking'.

34 Jesus replied, 'Surely you cannot make the bridegroom's attendants fast while the bridegroom is still with them?
35 But the time will come, the time for the bridegroom to be taken away from them; that will be the time when they will fast.'

36 He also told them this parable, 'No one tears a piece from a new cloak to put it on an old cloak; if he does, not only will he have torn the new one, but the piece taken from the new will not match the old.

37 'And nobody puts new wine into old skins; if he does, the new wine will burst the skins and then run out, and
38 the skins will be lost. ·No; new wine must be put into
39 fresh skins. ·And nobody who has been drinking old wine wants new. "The old is good" he says.'

Picking corn on the sabbath

1 6 Now one sabbath he happened to be taking a walk through the cornfields, and his disciples were picking ears of corn, rubbing them in their hands and
2 eating them. ·Some of the Pharisees said, 'Why are you doing something that is forbidden on the sabbath day?'
3 Jesus answered them, 'So you have not read what David did when he and his followers were hungry—
4 how he went into the house of God, took the loaves of offering and ate them and gave them to his followers,
5 loaves which only the priests are allowed to eat?' ·And he said to them, 'The Son of Man is master of the sabbath'.

Cure of the man with a withered hand

6 Now on another sabbath he went into the synagogue and began to teach, and a man was there whose right
7 hand was withered. ·The scribes and the Pharisees

37

were watching him to see if he would cure a man on the sabbath, hoping to find something to use against him. But he knew their thoughts; and he said to the man 8 with the withered hand, 'Stand up! Come out into the middle.' And he came out and stood there. ·Then Jesus 9 said to them, 'I put it to you: is it against the law on the sabbath to do good, or to do evil; to save life, or to destroy it?' ·Then he looked round at them all and said 10 to the man, 'Stretch out your hand'. He did so, and his hand was better. ·But they were furious, and began to 11 discuss the best way of dealing with Jesus.

The choice of the Twelve

Now it was about this time that he went out into the 12 hills to pray; and he spent the whole night in prayer to God. ·When day came he summoned his disciples and 13 picked out twelve of them; he called them 'apostles': Simon whom he called Peter, and his brother Andrew; 14 James, John, Philip, Bartholomew, ·Matthew, Thomas, 15 James son of Alphaeus, Simon called the Zealot, Judas son of James,[a] and Judas Iscariot who became a 16 traitor.

The crowds follow Jesus

He then came down with them and stopped at a piece 17 of level ground where there was a large gathering of his disciples with a great crowd of people from all parts of Judaea and from Jerusalem and from the coastal region of Tyre and Sidon ·who had come to hear him and to be 18 cured of their diseases. People tormented by unclean spirits were also cured, ·and everyone in the crowd was 19 trying to touch him because power came out of him that cured them all.

The inaugural discourse. The Beatitudes

20 Then fixing his eyes on his disciples he said:

'How happy are you who are poor: yours is the kingdom of God.

21 Happy you who are hungry now: you shall be satisfied.

Happy you who weep now: you shall laugh.

22 'Happy are you when people hate you, drive you out, abuse you, denounce your name as criminal, on account
23 of the Son of Man. ·Rejoice when that day comes and dance for joy, for then your reward will be great in heaven. This was the way their ancestors treated the prophets.

The curses

24 'But alas for you who are rich: you are having your consolation now.

25 Alas for you who have your fill now: you shall go hungry.

Alas for you who laugh now: you shall mourn and weep.

26 'Alas for you when the world speaks well of you! This was the way their ancestors treated the false prophets.

Love of enemies

27 'But I say this to you who are listening: Love your
28 enemies, do good to those who hate you, ·bless those
29 who curse you, pray for those who treat you badly. ·To the man who slaps you on one cheek, present the other cheek too; to the man who takes your cloak from you,
30 do not refuse your tunic. ·Give to everyone who asks you, and do not ask for your property back from the

6 a. Or possibly 'brother of James'.

man who robs you. ·Treat others as you would like them 31
to treat you. ·If you love those who love you, what 32
thanks can you expect? Even sinners love those who
love them. ·And if you do good to those who do good to 33
you, what thanks can you expect? For even sinners do that
much. ·And if you lend to those from whom you hope 34
to receive, what thanks can you expect? Even sinners
lend to sinners to get back the same amount. ·Instead, 35
love your enemies and do good, and lend without any
hope of return. You will have a great reward, and you
will be sons of the Most High, for he himself is kind to
the ungrateful and the wicked.

Compassion and generosity

'Be compassionate as your Father is compassionate. 36
Do not judge, and you will not be judged yourselves; 37
do not condemn, and you will not be condemned yourselves; grant pardon, and you will be pardoned. ·Give 38
and there will be gifts for you: a full measure, pressed
down, shaken together, and running over, will be
poured into your lap; because the amount you measure
out is the amount you will be given back.'

Integrity

He also told a parable to them, 'Can one blind man 39
guide another? Surely both will fall into a pit? ·The 40
disciple is not superior to his teacher; the fully trained
disciple will always be like his teacher. ·Why do you 41
observe the splinter in your brother's eye and never
notice the plank in your own? ·How can you say to your 42
brother, "Brother, let me take out the splinter that is in
your eye", when you cannot see the plank in your own?
Hypocrite! Take the plank out of your own eye first,

and then you will see clearly enough to take out the splinter that is in your brother's eye.

43 'There is no sound tree that produces rotten fruit,
44 nor again a rotten tree that produces sound fruit. ·For every tree can be told by its own fruit: people do not pick figs from thorns, nor gather grapes from brambles.
45 A good man draws what is good from the store of goodness in his heart; a bad man draws what is bad from the store of badness. For a man's words flow out of what fills his heart.

The true disciple

46 'Why do you call me, "Lord, Lord" and not do what I say?
47 'Everyone who comes to me and listens to my words
48 and acts on them—I will show you what he is like. ·He is like the man who when he built his house dug, and dug deep, and laid the foundations on rock; when the river was in flood it bore down on that house but could
49 not shake it, it was so well built. ·But the one who listens and does nothing is like the man who built his house on soil, with no foundations: as soon as the river bore down on it, it collapsed; and what a ruin that house became!'

Cure of the centurion's servant

1 7 When he had come to the end of all he wanted the
2 people to hear, he went into Capernaum. ·A centurion there had a servant, a favourite of his, who was
3 sick and near death. ·Having heard about Jesus he sent some Jewish elders to him to ask him to come and
4 heal his servant. ·When they came to Jesus they pleaded earnestly with him. 'He deserves this of you' they said
5 'because he is friendly towards our people; in fact, he
6 is the one who built the synagogue.' ·So Jesus went with

them, and was not very far from the house when the centurion sent word to him by some friends: 'Sir,' he said 'do not put yourself to trouble; because I am not worthy to have you under my roof; ·and for this same 7 reason I did not presume to come to you myself; but give the word and let my servant be cured. ·For I am under 8 authority myself, and have soldiers under me; and I say to one man: Go, and he goes; to another: Come here, and he comes; to my servant: Do this, and he does it.' When Jesus heard these words he was astonished at 9 him and, turning round, said to the crowd following him, 'I tell you, not even in Israel have I found faith like this'. ·And when the messengers got back to the house 10 they found the servant in perfect health.

The son of the widow of Nain restored to life

Now soon afterwards he went to a town called Nain, 11 accompanied by his disciples and a great number of people. ·When he was near the gate of the town it 12 happened that a dead man was being carried out for burial, the only son of his mother, and she was a widow. And a considerable number of the townspeople were with her. ·When the Lord*a* saw her he felt sorry for her. 13 'Do not cry' he said. ·Then he went up and put his hand 14 on the bier and the bearers stood still, and he said, 'Young man, I tell you to get up'. ·And the dead man 15 sat up and began to talk, and Jesus *gave him to his mother.b* ·Everyone was filled with awe and praised God 16 saying, 'A great prophet has appeared among us; God has visited his people'. ·And this opinion of him spread 17 throughout Judaea and all over the countryside.

The Baptist's question. Jesus commends him

The disciples of John gave him all this news, and 18

19 John, summoning two of his disciples, ·sent them to the Lord to ask, 'Are you the one who is to come, or must
20 we wait for someone else?' ·When the men reached Jesus they said, 'John the Baptist has sent us to you, to ask, "Are you the one who is to come or have we to wait for
21 someone else?"' ·It was just then that he cured many people of diseases and afflictions and of evil spirits, and
22 gave the gift of sight to many who were blind. ·Then he gave the messengers their answer, 'Go back and tell John what you have seen and heard: the blind see again, the lame walk, lepers are cleansed, and the deaf hear, the dead are raised to life, the Good News is proclaimed
23 to the poor ·and happy is the man who does not lose faith in me'.

24 When John's messengers had gone he began to talk
25 to the people about John, ·'What did you go out into the wilderness to see? A reed swaying in the breeze? No? Then what did you go out to see? A man dressed in fine clothes? Oh no, those who go in for fine clothes
26 and live luxuriously are to be found at court! ·Then what did you go out to see? A prophet? Yes, I tell you,
27 and much more than a prophet: ·he is the one of whom scripture says:

> See, I am going to send my messenger before you;
> he will prepare the way before you.[c]

28 'I tell you, of all the children born of women, there is no one greater than John; yet the least in the kingdom of
29 God is greater than he is.' ·All the people who heard him, and the tax collectors too, acknowledged God's plan by
30 accepting baptism from John; ·but by refusing baptism

7 a. For the first time in the gospel narrative Jesus is given the title hitherto reserved for God.
b. 1 K 17:23.   c. Ml 3:1.

from him the Pharisees and the lawyers had thwarted
what God had in mind for them.

Jesus condemns his contemporaries

'What description, then, can I find for the men of this 31
generation? What are they like? ·They are like children 32
shouting to one another while they sit in the market
place:

> "We played the pipes for you,
> and you wouldn't dance;
> we sang dirges,
> and you wouldn't cry".

'For John the Baptist comes, not eating bread, not 33
drinking wine, and you say, "He is possessed". ·The 34
Son of Man comes, eating and drinking, and you say,
"Look, a glutton and a drunkard, a friend of tax
collectors and sinners". ·Yet Wisdom has been proved 35
right by all her children.'

The woman who was a sinner

One of the Pharisees invited him to a meal. When he 36
arrived at the Pharisee's house and took his place at
table, ·a woman came in, who had a bad name in the 37
town. She had heard he was dining with the Pharisee
and had brought with her an alabaster jar of ointment.
She waited behind him at his feet, weeping, and her 38
tears fell on his feet, and she wiped them away with her
hair; then she covered his feet with kisses and anointed
them with the ointment.

When the Pharisee who had invited him saw this, he 39
said to himself, 'If this man were a prophet, he would
know who this woman is that is touching him and what

40 a bad name she has'. ·Then Jesus took him up and said, 'Simon, I have something to say to you'. 'Speak, Master'
41 was the reply. ·'There was once a creditor who had two men in his debt; one owed him five hundred denarii, the
42 other fifty. ·They were unable to pay, so he pardoned
43 them both. Which of them will love him more?' ·'The one who was pardoned more, I suppose' answered Simon. Jesus said, 'You are right'.

44 Then he turned to the woman. 'Simon,' he said 'you see this woman? I came into your house, and you poured no water over my feet, but she has poured out her tears
45 over my feet and wiped them away with her hair. ·You gave me no kiss, but she has been covering my feet with
46 kisses ever since I came in. ·You did not anoint my head with oil, but she has anointed my feet with ointment.
47 For this reason I tell you that her sins, her many sins, must have been forgiven her, or she would not have shown such great love. It is the man who is forgiven
48 little who shows little love.' ·Then he said to her, 'Your
49 sins are forgiven'. ·Those who were with him at table began to say to themselves, 'Who is this man, that he
50 even forgives sins?' ·But he said to the woman, 'Your faith has saved you; go in peace'.

The women accompanying Jesus

1 **8** Now after this he made his way through towns and villages preaching, and proclaiming the Good News
2 of the kingdom of God. With him went the Twelve, ·as well as certain women who had been cured of evil spirits and ailments: Mary surnamed the Magdalene, from
3 whom seven demons had gone out, ·Joanna the wife of Herod's steward Chuza, Susanna, and several others who provided for them out of their own resources.

Parable of the sower

With a large crowd gathering and people from every 4
town finding their way to him, he used this parable:

'A sower went out to sow his seed. As he sowed, some 5
fell on the edge of the path and was trampled on; and
the birds of the air ate it up. ·Some seed fell on rock, 6
and when it came up it withered away, having no
moisture. ·Some seed fell amongst thorns and the 7
thorns grew with it and choked it. ·And some seed fell 8
into rich soil and grew and produced its crop a hundred-
fold.' Saying this he cried, 'Listen, anyone who has ears
to hear!'

Why Jesus speaks in parables

His disciples asked him what this parable might mean, 9
and he said, 'The mysteries of the kingdom of God are 10
revealed to you; for the rest there are only parables, so
that

> *they may see but not perceive,*
> *listen but not understand.[a]*

The parable of the sower explained

'This, then, is what the parable means: the seed is the 11
word of God. ·Those on the edge of the path are people 12
who have heard it, and then the devil comes and carries
away the word from their hearts in case they should
believe and be saved. ·Those on the rock are people who, 13
when they first hear it, welcome the word with joy.
But these have no root; they believe for a while, and in
time of trial they give up. ·As for the part that fell into 14
thorns, this is people who have heard, but as they go on
their way they are choked by the worries and riches and
pleasures of life and do not reach maturity. ·As for the 15

part in the rich soil, this is people with a noble and generous heart who have heard the word and take it to themselves and yield a harvest through their perseverance.

Parable of the lamp

16 'No one lights a lamp to cover it with a bowl or to put it under a bed. No, he puts it on a lamp-stand so that
17 people may see the light when they come in. ·For nothing is hidden but it will be made clear, nothing secret but it
18 will be known and brought to light. ·So take care how you hear; for anyone who has will be given more; from anyone who has not, even what he thinks he has will be taken away.'

The true kinsmen of Jesus

19 His mother and his brothers came looking for him,
20 but they could not get to him because of the crowd. ·He was told, 'Your mother and brothers are standing out-
21 side and want to see you'. ·But he said in answer, 'My mother and my brothers are those who hear the word of God and put it into practice'.

The calming of the storm

22 One day, he got into a boat with his disciples and said to them, 'Let us cross over to the other side of the
23 lake'. So they put to sea, ·and as they sailed he fell asleep. When a squall came down on the lake the boat started taking in water and they found themselves in
24 danger. ·So they went to rouse him saying, 'Master! Master! We are going down!' Then he woke up and rebuked the wind and the rough water; and they sub-
25 sided and it was calm again. ·He said to them, 'Where

8 a. Is 6:9.

is your faith?' They were awestruck and astonished and said to one another, 'Who can this be, that gives orders even to winds and waves and they obey him?'

The Gerasene demoniac

They came to land in the country of the Gerasenes,[b] 26 which is opposite Galilee. ·He was stepping ashore when 27 a man from the town who was possessed by devils came towards him; for a long time the man had worn no clothes, nor did he live in a house, but in the tombs.

Catching sight of Jesus he gave a shout, fell at his feet 28 and cried out at the top of his voice, 'What do you want with me, Jesus, son of the Most High God? I implore you, do not torture me.' ·—For Jesus had been telling 29 the unclean spirit to come out of the man. It was a devil that had seized on him a great many times, and then they used to secure him with chains and fetters to restrain him, but he would always break the fastenings, and the devil would drive him out into the wilds. 'What is your name?' Jesus asked. 'Legion' he said— 30 because many devils had gone into him. ·And these 31 pleaded with him not to order them to depart into the Abyss.[c]

Now there was a large herd of pigs feeding there on 32 the mountain, and the devils pleaded with him to let them go into these. So he gave them leave. ·The devils 33 came out of the man and went into the pigs, and the herd charged down the cliff into the lake and were drowned.

When the swineherds saw what had happened they 34 ran off and told their story in the town and in the country round about; ·and the people went out to see 35 what had happened. When they came to Jesus they found the man from whom the devils had gone out sitting at the feet of Jesus, clothed and in his full senses; and they

36 were afraid. ·Those who had witnessed it told them how
the man who had been possessed came to be healed.
37 The entire population of the Gerasene territory was in
a state of panic and asked Jesus to leave them. So he
got into the boat and went back.
38   The man from whom the devils had gone out asked
to be allowed to stay with him, but he sent him away.
39 'Go back home,' he said 'and report all that God has
done for you.' So the man went off and spread throughout the town all that Jesus had done for him.

Cure of the woman with a haemorrhage. Jairus' daughter raised to life

40   On his return Jesus was welcomed by the crowd, for
41 they were all there waiting for him. ·And now there
came a man named Jarius, who was an official of the
synagogue. He fell at Jesus' feet and pleaded with him
42 to come to his house, ·because he had an only daughter
about twelve years old, who was dying. And the crowds
were almost stifling Jesus as he went.
43   Now there was a woman suffering from a haemorrhage for twelve years, whom no one had been able to
44 cure. ·She came up behind him and touched the fringe
of his cloak; and the haemorrhage stopped at that
45 instant. ·Jesus said, 'Who touched me?' When they all
denied that ·they had, Peter and his companions said,
46 'Master, it is the crowds round you, pushing'. ·But Jesus
said, 'Somebody touched me. I felt that power had gone
47 out from me.' ·Seeing herself discovered, the woman came
forward trembling, and falling at his feet explained in
front of all the people why she had touched him and how
48 she had been cured at that very moment. ·'My daughter,'

b. 'Gadarenes' in some versions.   **c.** The underworld.

he said 'your faith has restored you to health; go in peace.'

While he was still speaking, someone arrived from 49 the house of the synagogue official to say, 'Your daughter has died. Do not trouble the Master any further.' ·But Jesus had heard this, and he spoke to the 50 man, 'Do not be afraid, only have faith and she will be safe'. ·When he came to the house he allowed no one 51 to go in with him except Peter and John and James, and the child's father and mother. ·They were all weeping and 52 mourning for her, but Jesus said, 'Stop crying; she is not dead, but asleep'. ·But they laughed at him, knowing 53 she was dead. ·But taking her by the hand he called to 54 her, 'Child, get up'. ·And her spirit returned and she 55 got up at once. Then he told them to give her something to eat. ·Her parents were astonished, but he ordered 56 them not to tell anyone what had happened.

The mission of the Twelve

9 He called the Twelve together and gave them 1 power and authority over all devils and to cure diseases, ·and he sent them out to proclaim the king- 2 dom of God and to heal. ·He said to them, 'Take nothing 3 for the journey: neither staff, nor haversack, nor bread, nor money; and let none of you take a spare tunic. Whatever house you enter, stay there; and when you 4 leave, let it be from there. ·As for those who do not 5 welcome you, when you leave their town shake the dust from your feet as a sign to them.' ·So they set out 6 and went from village to village proclaiming the Good News and healing everywhere.

Herod and Jesus

Meanwhile Herod the tetrarch had heard about all 7

that was going on; and he was puzzled, because some people were saying that John had risen from the dead,
8 others that Elijah had reappeared, still others that one
9 of the ancient prophets had come back to life. ·But Herod said, 'John? I beheaded him. So who is this I hear such reports about?' And he was anxious to see him.

The return of the apostles. Miracle of the loaves

10 On their return the apostles gave him an account of all they had done. Then he took them with him and withdrew to a town called Bethsaida where they could be
11 by themselves. ·But the crowds got to know and they went after him. He made them welcome and talked to them about the kingdom of God; and he cured those who were in need of healing.

12 It was late afternoon when the Twelve came to him and said, 'Send the people away, and they can go to the villages and farms round about to find lodging and
13 food; for we are in a lonely place here'. ·He replied, 'Give them something to eat yourselves'. But they said, 'We have no more than five loaves and two fish, unless we are to go ourselves and buy food for all these
14 people'. ·For there were about five thousand men. But he said to his disciples, 'Get them to sit down in parties
15 of about fifty'. ·They did so and made them all sit down.
16 Then he took the five loaves and the two fish, raised his eyes to heaven, and said the blessing over them; then he broke them and handed them to his disciples to distri-
17 bute among the crowd. ·They all ate as much as they wanted, and when the scraps remaining were collected they filled twelve baskets.

51

Peter's profession of faith

Now one day when he was praying alone in the 18
presence of his disciples he put this question to them,
'Who do the crowds say I am?' ·And they answered, 19
'John the Baptist; others Elijah; and others say one of
the ancient prophets come back to life'. ·'But you,' he 20
said 'who do you say I am?' It was Peter who spoke up.
'The Christ of God' he said. ·But he gave them strict 21
orders not to tell anyone anything about this.

First prophecy of the Pasison

'The Son of Man' he said 'is destined to suffer 22
grievously, to be rejected by the elders and chief priests
and scribes and to be put to death, and to be raised up
on the third day.'

The condition of following Christ

Then to all he said, 'If anyone wants to be a follower 23
of mine, let him renounce himself and take up his cross
every day and follow me. ·For anyone who wants to 24
save his life will lose it; but anyone who loses his life
for my sake, that man will save it. ·What gain, then, is it 25
for a man to have won the whole world and to have lost
or ruined his very self? ·For if anyone is ashamed of me 26
and of my words, of him the Son of Man will be ashamed
when he comes in his own glory and in the glory of the
Father and the holy angels.

The kingdom will come soon

'I tell you truly, there are some standing here who 27
will not taste death before they see the kingdom of
God.'

The transfiguration

28 Now about eight days after this had been said, he took with him Peter and John and James and went up the
29 mountain to pray. ·As he prayed, the aspect of his face was changed and his clothing became brilliant as
30 lightning. ·Suddenly there were two men there talking
31 to him; they were Moses and Elijah ·appearing in glory, and they were speaking of his passing which he was to
32 accomplish in Jerusalem. ·Peter and his companions were heavy with sleep, but they kept awake and saw his
33 glory and the two men standing with him. ·As these were leaving him, Peter said to Jesus, 'Master, it is wonderful for us to be here; so let us make three tents, one for you, one for Moses and one for Elijah'.—He did
34 not know what he was saying. ·As he spoke, a cloud came and covered them with shadow; and when they went
35 into the cloud the disciples were afraid. ·And a voice came from the cloud saying, 'This is my Son, the
36 Chosen One. Listen to him.' ·And after the voice had spoken, Jesus was found alone. The disciples kept silence and, at that time, told no one what they had seen.

The epileptic demoniac

37 Now on the following day when they were coming down from the mountain a large crowd came to meet
38 him. ·Suddenly a man in the crowd cried out. 'Master,' he said 'I implore you to look at my son: he is my only
39 child. ·All at once a spirit will take hold of him, and give a sudden cry and throw the boy into convulsions with foaming at the mouth; it is slow to leave him, but
40 when it does it leaves the boy worn out. ·I begged your
41 disciples to cast it out, and they could not.' ·'Faithless and perverse generation!' Jesus said in reply 'How much

53

longer must I be among you and put up with you? Bring your son here.' ·The boy was still moving towards 42 Jesus when the devil threw him to the ground in convulsions. But Jesus rebuked the unclean spirit and cured the boy and gave him back to his father, ·and everyone 43 was awestruck by the greatness of God.

Second prophecy of the Passion

At a time when everyone was full of admiration for all he did, he said to his disciples, ·'For your part, you must 44 have these words constantly in your mind: The Son of Man is going to be handed over into the power of men'. ·But they did not understand him when he said 45 this; it was hidden from them so that they should not see the meaning of it, and they were afraid to ask him about what he had just said.

Who is the greatest?

An argument started between them about which of 46 them was the greatest. ·Jesus knew what thoughts were 47 going through their minds, and he took a little child and set him by his side ·and then said to them, 'Anyone 48 who welcomes this little child in my name welcomes me; and anyone who welcomes me welcomes the one who sent me. For the least among you all, that is the one who is great.'

On using the name of Jesus

John spoke up. 'Master,' he said 'we saw a man cast- 49 ing out devils in your name, and because he is not with us we tried to stop him.' ·But Jesus said to him, 'You 50 must not stop him: anyone who is not against you is for you'.

IV. THE JOURNEY TO JERUSALEM

A Samaritan village is inhospitable

51 Now as the time drew near for him to be taken up
to heaven, he resolutely took the road for Jerusalem
52 and sent messengers ahead of him. These set out, and
they went into a Samaritan village to make preparations
53 for him, ·but the people would not receive him because
54 he was making for Jersualem.ᵃ ·Seeing this, the disciples
James and John said, 'Lord, do you want us to call
55 down fire from heaven to burn them up?' ·But he turned
56 and rebuked them, ·and they went off to another village.

Hardships of the apostolic calling

57 As they travelled along they met a man on the road
who said to him, 'I will follow you wherever you go'.
58 Jesus answered, 'Foxes have holes and the birds of the
air have nests, but the Son of Man has nowhere to lay
his head'.

59 Another to whom he said, 'Follow me', replied, 'Let
60 me go and bury my father first'. ·But he answered,
'Leave the dead to bury their dead; your duty is to go
and spread the news of the kingdom of God'.

61 Another said, 'I will follow you, sir, but first let me go
62 and say good-bye to my people at home'. ·Jesus said to
him, 'Once the hand is laid on the plough, no one who
looks back is fit for the kingdom of God'.

The mission of the seventy-two disciples

1 **10** After this the Lord appointed seventy-two
others and sent them out ahead of him, in

9 a. The hatred of Samaritans for Jews would show itself particularly towards those who were on pilgrimage to Jerusalem.

pairs, to all the towns and places he himself was to visit. ·He said to them, 'The harvest is rich but the 2 labourers are few, so ask the Lord of the harvest to send labourers to his harvest. ·Start off now, but remember, 3 I am sending you out like lambs among wolves. ·Carry 4 no purse, no haversack, no sandals. Salute no one on the road. ·Whatever house you go into, let your first words 5 be, "Peace to this house!" ·And if a man of peace lives 6 there, your peace will go and rest on him; if not, it will come back to you. ·Stay in the same house, taking what 7 food and drink they have to offer, for the labourer deserves his wages; do not move from house to house. Whenever you go into a town where they make you 8 welcome, eat what is set before you. ·Cure those in it 9 who are sick, and say, "The kingdom of God is very near to you". ·But whenever you enter a town and they 10 do not make you welcome, go out into its streets and say, ·"We wipe off the very dust of your town that 11 clings to our feet, and leave it with you. Yet be sure of this: the kingdom of God is very near." ·I tell you, on 12 that day it will not go as hard with Sodom as with that town.

'Alas for you, Chorazin! Alas for you, Bethsaida! For 13 if the miracles done in you had been done in Tyre and Sidon, they would have repented long ago, sitting in sackcloth and ashes. ·And still, it will not go as hard 14 with Tyre and Sidon at the Judgement as with you. And as for you, Capernaum, did you want to be 15 exalted high as heaven? *You shall be thrown down to hell.*[a]

'Anyone who listens to you listens to me; anyone 16 who rejects you rejects me, and those who reject me reject the one who sent me.'

True cause for the apostles to rejoice

17 The seventy-two came back rejoicing. 'Lord,' they
said 'even the devils submit to us when we use your
18 name.' ·He said to them, 'I watched Satan fall like
19 lightning from heaven. ·Yes, I have given you power to
tread underfoot serpents and scorpions and the whole
20 strength of the enemy; nothing shall ever hurt you. ·Yet
do not rejoice that the spirits submit to you; rejoice
rather that your names are written in heaven.'

The Good News revealed to the simple. The Father and the Son

21 It was then that, filled with joy by the Holy Spirit, he
said, 'I bless you, Father, Lord of heaven and of earth,
for hiding these things from the learned and the clever
and revealing them to mere children. Yes, Father, for
22 that is what it pleased you to do. ·Everything has been
entrusted to me by my Father; and no one knows who
the Son is except the Father, and who the Father is
except the Son and those to whom the Son chooses to
reveal him.'

The privilege of the disciples

23 Then turning to his disciples he spoke to them in
24 private, 'Happy the eyes that see what you see, ·for I tell
you that many prophets and kings wanted to see what
you see, and never saw it: to hear what you hear, and
never heard it'.

The great commandment

25 There was a lawyer who, to disconcert him, stood up
and said to him, 'Master what must I do to inherit

10 a. See Is 14:13, 15.

eternal life?' ·He said to him, 'What is written in the 26
Law? What do you read there?' ·He replied, '*You must* 27
love the Lord your God with all your heart, with all your
soul, with all your strength, and with all your mind, *and*
your neighbour as yourself'.[b] ·'You have answered right,' 28
said Jesus 'do this and life is yours.'

Parable of the good Samaritan

But the man was anxious to justify himself and said to 29
Jesus, 'And who is my neighbour?' ·Jesus replied, 'A 30
man was once on his way down from Jerusalem to
Jericho and fell into the hands of brigands; they took all
he had, beat him and then made off, leaving him half
dead. ·Now a priest happened to be travelling down the 31
same road, but when he saw the man, he passed by on
the other side. ·In the same way a Levite who came to the 32
place saw him, and passed by on the other side. ·But a 33
Samaritan traveller who came upon him was moved
with compassion when he saw him. ·He went up and 34
bandaged his wounds, pouring oil and wine on them.
He then lifted him on to his own mount, carried him to
the inn and looked after him. ·Next day, he took out two 35
denarii and handed them to the innkeeper. "Look after
him," he said "and on my way back I will make good
any extra expense you have." ·Which of these three, 36
do you think, proved himself a neighbour to the man
who fell into the brigands' hands?' ·'The one who took 37
pity on him' he replied. Jesus said to him, 'Go, and do
the same yourself'.

Martha and Mary

In the course of their journey he came to a village, 38
and a woman named Martha welcomed him into her
house. ·She had a sister called Mary, who sat down at 39

40 the Lord's feet and listened to him speaking. ·Now Martha who was distracted with all the serving said, 'Lord, do you not care that my sister is leaving me to do the serving all by myself? Please tell her to help me.'
41 But the Lord answered: 'Martha, Martha,' he said 'you
42 worry and fret about so many things, ·and yet few are needed, indeed only one. It is Mary who has chosen the better part; it is not to be taken from her.'

The Lord's prayer

1 **11** Now once he was in a certain place praying, and when he had finished one of his disciples said, 'Lord, teach us to pray, just as John taught his disciples'.
2 He said to them, 'Say this when you pray:

"Father, may your name be held holy,
your kingdom come;
3 give us each day our daily bread,
and forgive us our sins,
4 for we ourselves forgive each one who is in debt to us.
And do not put us to the test." '

The importunate friend

5 He also said to them, 'Suppose one of you has a friend and goes to him in the middle of the night to say, "My
6 friend, lend me three loaves, ·because a friend of mine on his travels has just arrived at my house and I have
7 nothing to offer him"; ·and the man answers from inside the house, "Do not bother me. The door is bolted now, and my children and I are in bed; I cannot get up to give
8 it you". ·I tell you, if the man does not get up and give it him for friendship's sake, persistence will be enough to make him get up and give his friend all he wants.

b. Dt 6:5 and Lv 19:18.

Effective prayer

'So I say to you: Ask, and it will be given to you; 9
search, and you will find; knock, and the door will be
opened to you. ·For the one who asks always receives; 10
the one who searches always finds; the one who knocks
will always have the door opened to him. ·What father 11
among you would hand his son a stone when he asked
for bread? Or hand him a snake instead of a fish? ·Or 12
hand him a scorpion if he asked for an egg? ·If you then, 13
who are evil, know how to give your children what is
good, how much more will the heavenly Father give the
Holy Spirit to those who ask him!'

Jesus and Beelzebul

He was casting out a devil and it was dumb; but when 14
the devil had gone out the dumb man spoke, and the
people were amazed. ·But some of them said, 'It is 15
through Beelzebul, the prince of devils, that he casts
out devils'. ·Others asked him, as a test, for a sign from 16
heaven; ·but, knowing what they were thinking, he said 17
to them, 'Every kingdom divided against itself is heading
for ruin, and a household divided against itself collapses.
So too with Satan: if he is divided against himself, how 18
can his kingdom stand?—Since you assert that it is
through Beelzebul that I cast out devils. ·Now if it is 19
through Beelzebul that I cast out devils, through whom
do your own experts cast them out? Let them be your
judges, then. ·But if it is through the finger of God that 20
I cast out devils, then know that the kingdom of God
has overtaken you. ·So long as a strong man fully armed 21
guards his own palace, his goods are undisturbed; ·but 22
when someone stronger than he is attacks and defeats
him, the stronger man takes away all the weapons he
relied on and shares out his spoil.

No compromise

23 'He who is not with me is against me; and he who does not gather with me scatters.

Return of the unclean spirit

24 'When an unclean spirit goes out of a man it wanders through waterless country looking for a place to rest, and not finding one it says, "I will go back to the home
25 I came from". ·But on arrival, finding it swept and
26 tidied, ·it then goes off and brings seven other spirits more wicked than itself, and they go in and set up house there, so that the man ends up by being worse than he was before.'

The truly happy

27 Now as he was speaking, a woman in the crowd raised
28 her voice and said, ·'Happy the womb that bore you and the breasts you sucked!' ·But he replied, 'Still happier those who hear the word of God and keep it!'

The sign of Jonah

29 The crowds got even bigger and he addressed them, 'This is a wicked generation; it is asking for a sign. The
30 only sign it will be given is the sign of Jonah. ·For just as Jonah became a sign to the Ninevites, so will the Son of
31 Man be to this generation. ·On Judgement day the Queen of the South will rise up with the men of this generation and condemn them, because she came from the ends of the earth to hear the wisdom of Solomon;
32 and there is something greater than Solomon here. ·On Judgement day the men of Nineveh will stand up with this generation and condemn it, because when Jonah preached they repented; and there is something greater than Jonah here.

The parable of the lamp repeated

'No one lights a lamp and puts it in some hidden 33
place or under a tub, but on the lamp-stand so that
people may see the light when they come in. ·The lamp 34
of your body is your eye. When your eye is sound, your
whole body too is filled with light; but when it is
diseased your body too will be all darkness. ·See to it 35
then that the light inside you is not darkness. ·If, there- 36
fore, your whole body is filled with light, and no trace of
darkness, it will be light entirely, as when the lamp shines
on you with its rays.'

The Pharisees and the lawyers attacked

He had just finished speaking when a Pharisee 37
invited him to dine at his house. He went in and sat
down at the table. ·The Pharisee saw this and was 38
surprised that he had not first washed before the meal.
But the Lord said to him, 'Oh, you Pharisees! You 39
clean the outside of cup and plate, while inside yourselves you are filled with extortion and wickedness.
Fools! Did not he who made the outside make the 40
inside too? ·Instead, give alms from what you have and 41
then indeed everything will be clean for you. ·But alas 42
for you Pharisees! You who pay your tithe of mint and
rue and all sorts of garden herbs and overlook justice
and the love of God! These you should have practised,
without leaving the others undone. ·Alas for you 43
Pharisees who like taking the seats of honour in the
synagogues and being greeted obsequiously in the
market squares! ·Alas for you, because you are like the 44
unmarked tombs that men walk on without knowing
it!*a*

A lawyer then spoke up. 'Master,' he said 'when 45
you speak like this you insult us too.' ·'Alas for you 46

lawyers also,' he replied 'because you load on men burdens that are unendurable, burdens that you yourselves do not move a finger to lift.

47 'Alas for you who build the tombs of the prophets,
48 the men your ancestors killed! ·In this way you both witness what your ancestors did and approve it; they did the killing, you do the building.

49 'And that is why the Wisdom of God said, "I will send them prophets and apostles; some they will
50 slaughter and persecute, ·so that this generation will have to answer for every prophet's blood that has been
51 shed since the foundation of the world, ·from the blood of Abel to the blood of Zechariah, who was murdered between the altar and the sanctuary". Yes, I tell you, this generation will have to answer for it all.

52 'Alas for you lawyers who have taken away the key of knowledge! You have not gone in yourselves, and have prevented others going in who wanted to.'

53 When he left the house, the scribes and the Pharisees began a furious attack on him and tried to force answers
54 from him on innumerable questions, ·setting traps to catch him out in something he might say.

Open and fearless speech

1 **12** Meanwhile the people had gathered in their thousands so that they were treading on one another. And he began to speak, first of all to his disciples. 'Be on your guard against the yeast of the
2 Pharisees—that is, their hypocrisy. ·Everything that is now covered will be uncovered, and everything now
3 hidden will be made clear. ·For this reason, whatever you have said in the dark will be heard in the daylight,

11 a. Thus contracting legal impurity, Nb 19:16.

and what you have whispered in hidden places will be proclaimed on the housetops.

'To you my friends I say: Do not be afraid of those 4 who kill the body and after that can do no more. ·I will 5 tell you whom to fear: fear him who, after he has killed, has the power to cast into hell. Yes, I tell you, fear him. Can you not buy five sparrows for two pennies? And 6 yet not one is forgotten in God's sight. ·Why, every hair 7 on your head has been counted. There is no need to be afraid: you are worth more than hundreds of sparrows.

'I tell you, if anyone openly declares himself for me 8 in the presence of men, the Son of Man will declare himself for him in the presence of God's angels. ·But 9 the man who disowns me in the presence of men will be disowned in the presence of God's angels.

'Everyone who says a word against the Son of Man 10 will be forgiven, but he who blasphemes against the Holy Spirit will not be forgiven.

'When they take you before synagogues and magis- 11 trates and authorities, do not worry about how to defend yourselves or what to say, ·because when the 12 time comes, the Holy Spirit will teach you what you must say.'

On hoarding possessions

A man in the crowd said to him, 'Master, tell my 13 brother to give me a share of our inheritance'. ·'My 14 friend,' he replied 'who appointed me your judge, or the arbitrator of your claims?' ·Then he said to them, 15 'Watch, and be on your guard against avarice of any kind, for a man's life is not made secure by what he owns, even when he has more than he needs'.

Then he told them a parable: 'There was once a rich 16 man who, having had a good harvest from his land,

17 thought to himself, "What am I to do? I have not
18 enough room to store my crops." ·Then he said, "This
is what I will do: I will pull down my barns and build
bigger ones, and store all my grain and my goods in
19 them, ·and I will say to my soul: My soul, you have
plenty of good things laid by for many years to come;
20 take things easy, eat, drink, have a good time". ·But
God said to him, "Fool! This very night the demand
will be made for your soul; and this hoard of yours,
21 whose will it be then?" ·So it is when a man stores up
treasure for himself in place of making himself rich in
the sight of God.'

Trust in Providence

22 Then he said to his disciples, 'That is why I am telling
you not to worry about your life and what you are to
eat, nor about your body and how you are to clothe it.
23 For life means more than food, and the body more than
24 clothing. ·Think of the ravens. They do not sow or reap;
they have no storehouses and no barns; yet God feeds
them. And how much more are you worth than the
25 birds! ·Can any of you, for all his worrying, add a single
26 cubit to his span of life? ·If the smallest things, therefore,
are outside your control, why worry about the rest?
27 Think of the flowers; they never have to spin or weave;
yet, I assure you, not even Solomon in all his regalia
28 was robed like one of these. ·Now if that is how God
clothes the grass in the field which is there today and
thrown into the furnace tomorrow, how much more will
29 he look after you, you men of little faith! ·But you,
you must not set your hearts on things to eat and things
30 to drink; nor must you worry. ·It is the pagans of this
world who set their hearts on all these things. Your
31 Father well knows you need them. ·No; set your hearts

65

on his kingdom, and these other things will be given you as well.

'There is no need to be afraid, little flock, for it has 32 pleased your Father to give you the kingdom.

On almsgiving

'Sell your possessions and give alms. Get yourselves 33 purses that do not wear out, treasure that will not fail you, in heaven where no thief can reach it and no moth destroy it. ·For where your treasure is, there will your 34 heart be also.

On being ready for the Master's return

'See that you are dressed for action and have your 35 lamps lit. ·Be like men waiting for their master to return 36 from the wedding feast, ready to open the door as soon as he comes and knocks. ·Happy those servants whom 37 the master finds awake when he comes. I tell you solemnly, he will put on an apron, sit them down at table and wait on them. ·It may be in the second watch 38 he comes, or in the third, but happy those servants if he finds them ready. ·You may be quite sure of this, that if 39 the householder had known at what hour the burglar would come, he would not have let anyone break through the wall of his house. ·You too must stand ready, because 40 the Son of Man is coming at an hour you do not expect.'

Peter said, 'Lord, do you mean this parable for us, 41 or for everyone?' ·The Lord replied, 'What sort of 42 steward,[a] then, is faithful and wise enough for the master to place him over his household to give them their allowance of food at the proper time? ·Happy that 43 servant if his master's arrival finds him at this employment. ·I tell you truly, he will place him over everything 44 he owns. ·But as for the servant who says to himself, 45

"My master is taking his time coming", and sets about beating the menservants and the maids, and eating and
46 drinking and getting drunk, ·his master will come on a day he does not expect and at an hour he does not know. The master will cut him off and send him to the same fate as the unfaithful.
47 'The servant who knows what his master wants, but has not even started to carry out those wishes, will
48 receive very many strokes of the lash. ·The one who did not know, but deserves to be beaten for what he has done, will receive fewer strokes. When a man has had a great deal given him, a great deal will be demanded of him; when a man has had a great deal given him on trust, even more will be expected of him.

Jesus and his Passion

49 'I have come to bring fire to the earth, and how I wish
50 it were blazing already! ·There is a baptism I must still receive, and how great is my distress till it is over!

Jesus the cause of dissension

51 'Do you suppose that I am here to bring peace on
52 earth? No, I tell you, but rather division. ·For from now on a household of five will be divided: three against
53 two and two against three; ·the father divided against the son, son against father, mother against daughter, daughter against mother, mother-in-law against daughter-in-law, daughter-in-law against mother-in-law.'

On reading the signs of the times

54 He said again to the crowds, 'When you see a cloud looming up in the west you say at once that rain is

12 a. I.e. a servant or employee with authority to act as his master's deputy in his absence.

coming, and so it does. ·And when the wind is from the 55
south you say it will be hot, and it is. ·Hypocrites! You 56
know how to interpret the face of the earth and the
sky. How is it you do not know how to interpret these
times?

'Why not judge for yourselves what is right? ·For 57,58
example: when you go to court with your opponent, try
to settle with him on the way, or he may drag you before
the judge and the judge hand you over to the bailiff
and the bailiff have you thrown into prison. ·I tell you, 59
you will not get out till you have paid the very last
penny.'

Examples inviting repentance

13 It was just about this time that some people arrived 1
and told him about the Galileans whose blood
Pilate had mingled with that of their sacrifices.ᵃ ·At this 2
he said to them, 'Do you suppose these Galileans who
suffered like that were greater sinners than any other
Galileans? ·They were not, I tell you. No; but unless 3
you repent you will all perish as they did. ·Or those 4
eighteen on whom the tower at Siloam fell and killed
them? Do you suppose that they were more guilty than
all the other people living in Jerusalem? ·They were not, 5
I tell you. No; but unless you repent you will all perish
as they did.'

Parable of the barren fig tree

He told this parable: 'A man had a fig tree planted in 6
his vineyard, and he came looking for fruit on it but
found none. ·He said to the man who looked after the 7
vineyard, "Look here, for three years now I have been
coming to look for fruit on this fig tree and finding
none. Cut it down: why should it be taking up the

68

8 ground?" ·"Sir," the man replied "leave it one more
9 year and give me time to dig round it and manure it: ·it
may bear fruit next year; if not, then you can cut it
down." '

Healing of the crippled woman on a sabbath

10   One sabbath day he was teaching in one of the
11 synagogues, ·and a woman was there who for eighteen
years had been possessed by a spirit that left her
enfeebled; she was bent double and quite unable to
12 stand upright. ·When Jesus saw her he called her over
13 and said, 'Woman, you are rid of your infirmity' ·and he
laid his hands on her. And at once she straightened up,
and she glorified God.

14   But the synagogue official was indignant because Jesus
had healed on the sabbath, and he addressed the people
present. 'There are six days' he said 'when work is to be
done. Come and be healed on one of those days and
15 not on the sabbath.' ·But the Lord answered him.
'Hypocrites!' he said 'Is there one of you who does not
untie his ox or his donkey from the manger on the
16 sabbath and take it out for watering? ·And this woman,
a daughter of Abraham whom Satan has held bound
these eighteen years—was it not right to untie her bonds
17 on the sabbath day?' ·When he said this, all his adver-
saries were covered with confusion, and all the people
were overjoyed at all the wonders he worked.

Parable of the mustard seed

18   He went on to say, 'What is the kingdom of God like?
19 What shall I compare it with? ·It is like a mustard seed

13 a. The author expects this incident, and that mentioned in
v. 4, to be known to his readers; no other evidence of them
remains.

which a man took and threw into his garden: it grew
and became a tree, and the birds of the air sheltered in
its branches.'

Parable of the yeast

Another thing he said, 'What shall I compare the 20
kingdom of God with? ·It is like the yeast a woman took 21
and mixed in with three measures of flour till it was
leavened all through.'

The narrow door; rejection of the Jews, call of the gentiles

Through towns and villages he went teaching, making 22
his way to Jerusalem. ·Someone said to him, 'Sir, will 23
there be only a few saved?' He said to them, ·'Try your 24
best to enter by the narrow door, because, I tell you,
many will try to enter and will not succeed.

'Once the master of the house has got up and locked 25
the door, you may find yourself knocking on the door,
saying, "Lord, open to us" but he will answer, "I do
not know where you come from". ·Then you will find 26
yourself saying, "We once ate and drank in your company; you taught in our streets" ·but he will reply, "I 27
do not know where you come from. *Away from me, all
you wicked men!"* [b]

'Then there will be weeping and grinding of teeth, 28
when you see Abraham and Isaac and Jacob and all
the prophets in the kingdom of God, and yourselves
turned outside. ·And men from east and west, from 29
north and south, will come to take their places at the
feast in the kingdom of God.

'Yes, there are those now last who will be first, and 30
those now first who will be last.'

Herod the fox

31 Just at this time some Pharisees came up. 'Go away' they said. 'Leave this place, because Herod means to
32 kill you.' ·He replied, 'You may go and give that fox this message: Learn that today and tomorrow I cast out
33 devils and on the third day[c] attain my end. ·But for today and tomorrow and the next day I must go on, since it would not be right for a prophet to die outside Jerusalem.

Jerusalem admonished

34 'Jerusalem, Jerusalem, you that kill the prophets and stone those who are sent to you! How often have I longed to gather your children, as a hen gathers her
35 brood under her wings, and you refused! ·So be it! Your house will be left to you. Yes, I promise you, you shall not see me till the time comes when you say: *Blessings on him who comes in the name of the Lord!*[d]

Healing of a dropsical man on the sabbath

1 **14** Now on a sabbath day he had gone for a meal to the house of one of the leading Pharisees; and
2 they watched him closely. ·There in front of him was a
3 man with dropsy, ·and Jesus addressed the lawyers and Pharisees. 'Is it against the law' he asked 'to cure a man
4 on the sabbath, or not?' ·But they remained silent, so he
5 took the man and cured him and sent him away. ·Then he said to them, 'Which of you here, if his son falls into a well, or his ox, will not pull him out on a sabbath day
6 without hesitation?' ·And to this they could find no answer.

b. Ps 6:8.   **c.** 'after a short time'.   **d.** Ps 118:26.

71

On choosing places at table

He then told the guests a parable, because he had 7
noticed how they picked the places of honour. He said
this, ·'When someone invites you to a wedding feast, do 8
not take your seat in the place of honour. A more
distinguished person than you may have been invited,
and the person who invited you both may come and 9
say, "Give up your place to this man". And then, to
your embarrassment, you would have to go and take
the lowest place. ·No; when you are a guest, make your 10
way to the lowest place and sit there, so that, when your
host comes, he may say, "My friend, move up higher".
In that way, everyone with you at the table will see you
honoured. ·For everyone who exalts himself will be 11
humbled, and the man who humbles himself will be
exalted.'

On choosing guests to be invited

Then he said to his host, 'When you give a lunch or a 12
dinner, do not ask your friends, brothers, relations or
rich neighbours, for fear they repay your courtesy by
inviting you in return. ·No; when you have a party, 13
invite the poor, the crippled, the lame, the blind; ·that 14
they cannot pay you back means that you are fortunate,
because repayment will be made to you when the virtuous rise again.'

The invited guests who made excuses

On hearing this, one of those gathered round the table 15
said to him, 'Happy the man who will be at the feast in
the kingdom of God!' ·But he said to him, 'There was a 16
man who gave a great banquet, and he invited a large
number of people. ·When the time for the banquet came, 17
he sent his servant to say to those who had been invited,

18 "Come along: everything is ready now". ·But all alike started to make excuses. The first said, "I have bought a piece of land and must go and see it. Please accept my
19 apologies." ·Another said, "I have bought five yoke of oxen and am on my way to try them out. Please accept
20 my apologies." ·Yet another said, "I have just got married and so am unable to come".
21 'The servant returned and reported this to his master. Then the householder, in a rage, said to his servant, "Go out quickly into the streets and alleys of the town and bring in here the poor, the crippled, the blind and
22 the lame". ·"Sir," said the servant "your orders have
23 been carried out and there is still room." ·Then the master said to his servant, "Go to the open roads and the hedgerows and force people to come in to make sure my
24 house is full; ·because, I tell you, not one of those who were invited shall have a taste of my banquet".'

Renouncing all that one holds dear

25 Great crowds accompanied him on his way and he
26 turned and spoke to them. ·'If any man comes to me without hating*a* his father, mother, wife, children, brothers, sisters, yes and his own life too, he cannot be
27 my disciple. ·Anyone who does not carry his cross and come after me cannot be my disciple.

Renouncing possessions

28 'And indeed, which of you here, intending to build a tower, would not first sit down and work out the cost to
29 see if he had enough to complete it? ·Otherwise, if he laid the foundation and then found himself unable to finish the work, the onlookers would all start making

14 a. Hebraism: an emphatic way of expressing a total detachment.

73

fun of him and saying, ·"Here is a man who started to 30
build and was unable to finish". ·Or again, what king 31
marching to war against another king would not first sit
down and consider whether with ten thousand men he
could stand up to the other who advanced against him
with twenty thousand? ·If not, then while the other king 32
was still a long way off, he would send envoys to sue for
peace. ·So in the same way, none of you can be my 33
disciple unless he gives up all his possessions.

On loss of enthusiasm in a disciple

'Salt is a useful thing. But if the salt itself loses its 34
taste, how can it be seasoned again? ·It is good for 35
neither soil nor manure heap. People throw it out.
Listen, anyone who has ears to hear!'

The three parables of God's mercy

15 The tax collectors and the sinners, meanwhile, 1
were all seeking his company to hear what he had
to say, ·and the Pharisees and the scribes complained. 2
'This man' they said 'welcomes sinners and eats with
them.' ·So he spoke this parable to them: 3

The lost sheep

'What man among you with a hundred sheep, losing 4
one, would not leave the ninety-nine in the wilderness
and go after the missing one till he found it? ·And when 5
he found it, would he not joyfully take it on his shoulders
and then, when he got home, call together his friends 6
and neighbours? "Rejoice with me," he would say "I
have found my sheep that was lost." ·In the same way, 7
I tell you, there will be more rejoicing in heaven over
one repentant sinner than over ninety-nine virtuous
men who have no need of repentance.

The lost drachma

8 'Or again, what woman with ten drachmas would not, if she lost one, light a lamp and sweep out the house and
9 search thoroughly till she found it? ·And then, when she had found it, call together her friends and neighbours? "Rejoice with me," she would say "I have found the
10 drachma I lost." ·In the same way, I tell you, there is rejoicing among the angels of God over one repentant sinner.'

The lost son (the 'prodigal') and the dutiful son

11,12 He also said, 'A man had two sons. ·The younger said to his father, "Father, let me have the share of the estate that would come to me". So the father divided the
13 property between them. ·A few days later, the younger son got together everything he had and left for a distant country where he squandered his money on a life of debauchery.

14 'When he had spent it all, that country experienced a
15 severe famine, and now he began to feel the pinch, ·so he hired himself out to one of the local inhabitants who
16 put him on his farm to feed the pigs. ·And he would willingly have filled his belly with the husks the pigs
17 were eating but no one offered him anything. ·Then he came to his senses and said, "How many of my father's paid servants have more food than they want, and here
18 am I dying of hunger! ·I will leave this place and go to my father and say: Father, I have sinned against
19 heaven and against you; ·I no longer deserve to be called your son; treat me as one of your paid servants."
20 So he left the place and went back to his father.

'While he was still a long way off, his father saw him and was moved with pity. He ran to the boy, clasped
21 him in his arms and kissed him tenderly. ·Then his son

said, "Father, I have sinned against heaven and against you. I no longer deserve to be called your son." ·But 22 the father said to his servants, "Quick! Bring out the best robe and put it on him; put a ring on his finger and sandals on his feet. ·Bring the calf we have been fatten- 23 ing, and kill it; we are going to have a feast, a celebra- tion, ·because this son of mine was dead and has come 24 back to life; he was lost and is found." And they began to celebrate.

'Now the elder son was out in the fields, and on his 25 way back, as he drew near the house, he could hear music and dancing. ·Calling one of the servants he 26 asked what it was all about. ·"Your brother has come" 27 replied the servant "and your father has killed the calf we had fattened because he has got him back safe and sound." ·He was angry then and refused to go in, and 28 his father came out to plead with him; ·but he answered 29 his father, "Look, all these years I have slaved for you and never once disobeyed your orders, yet you never offered me so much as a kid for me to celebrate with my friends. ·But, for this son of yours, when he comes back 30 after swallowing up your property—he and his women —you kill the calf we had been fattening."

'The father said, "My son, you are with me always 31 and all I have is yours. ·But it was only right we should 32 celebrate and rejoice, because your brother here was dead and has come to life; he was lost and is found." '

The crafty steward

16 He also said to his disciples, 'There was a rich man 1 and he had a steward who was denounced to him for being wasteful with his property. ·He called for the 2 man and said, "What is this I hear about you? Draw me up an account of your stewardship because you are

3 not to be my steward any longer." ·Then the steward said to himself, "Now that my master is taking the stewardship from me, what am I to do? Dig? I am not strong enough. Go begging? I should be too ashamed.

4 Ah, I know what I will do to make sure that when I am dismissed from office there will be some to welcome me into their homes."

5 'Then he called his master's debtors one by one. To the first, he said, "How much do you owe my master?"

6 "One hundred measures of oil" was the reply. The steward said, "Here, take your bond; sit down straight

7 away and write fifty". ·To another he said, "And you, sir, how much do you owe?" "One hundred measures of wheat" was the reply. The steward said, "Here, take your bond and write eighty".

8 'The master praised the dishonest steward for his astuteness.[a] For the children of this world are more astute in dealing with their own kind than are the children of light.'

The right use of money

9 'And so I tell you this: use money, tainted as it is, to win you friends, and thus make sure that when it fails you, they will welcome you into the tents of eternity.

10 The man who can be trusted in little things can be trusted in great; the man who is dishonest in little things

11 will be dishonest in great. ·If then you cannot be trusted with money, that tainted thing, who will trust you with

12 genuine riches? ·And if you cannot be trusted with what is not yours, who will give you what is your very own?

13 'No servant can be the slave of two masters: he will

16 a. Not for his dishonesty.

either hate the first and love the second, or treat the first with respect and the second with scorn. You cannot be the slave both of God and of money.'

Against the Pharisees and their love of money

The Pharisees, who loved money, heard all this and 14 laughed at him. ·He said to them, 'You are the very ones 15 who pass yourselves off as virtuous in people's sight, but God knows your hearts. For what is thought highly of by men is loathsome in the sight of God.

The kingdom stormed

'Up to the time of John it was the law and the 16 Prophets; since then, the kingdom of God has been preached, and by violence everyone is getting in.

The Law remains

'It is easier for heaven and earth to disappear than for 17 one little stroke to drop out of the Law.

Marriage indissoluble

'Everyone who divorces his wife and marries another 18 is guilty of adultery, and the man who marries a woman divorced by her husband commits adultery.

The rich man and Lazarus

'There was a rich man who used to dress in purple and 19 fine linen and feast magnificently every day. ·And at his 20 gate there lay a poor man called Lazarus, covered with sores, ·who longed to fill himself with the scraps that 21 fell from the rich man's table. Dogs even came and licked his sores. ·Now the poor man died and was carried 22 away by the angels to the bosom of Abraham. The rich man also died and was buried.

23 'In his torment in Hades he looked up and saw
24 Abraham a long way off with Lazarus in his bosom. ·So
he cried out, "Father Abraham, pity me and send
Lazarus to dip the tip of his finger in water and cool
25 my tongue, for I am in agony in these flames". ·"My
son," Abraham replied "remember that during your life
good things came your way, just as bad things came the
way of Lazarus. Now he is being comforted here while
26 you are in agony. ·But that is not all: between us and
you a great gulf has been fixed, to stop anyone, if he
wanted to, crossing from our side to yours, and to stop
any crossing from your side to ours."

27 'The rich man replied, "Father, I beg you then to
28 send Lazarus to my father's house, ·since I have five
brothers, to give them warning so that they do not come
29 to this place of torment too". ·"They have Moses and
the prophets," said Abraham "let them listen to them."
30 "Ah no, father Abraham," said the rich man "but if
someone comes to them from the dead, they will
31 repent." ·Then Abraham said to him, "If they will not
listen either to Moses or to the prophets, they will not
be convinced even if someone should rise from the
dead".'

On leading others astray

1 **17** He said to his disciples, 'Obstacles are sure to
come, but alas for the one who provides them!
2 It would be better for him to be thrown into the sea
with a millstone put round his neck than that he should
3 lead astray a single one of these little ones. ·Watch
yourselves!

Brotherly correction

'If your brother does something wrong, reprove him

and, if he is sorry, forgive him. ·And if he wrongs you 4
seven times a day and seven times comes back to you
and says, "I am sorry", you must forgive him.'

The power of faith

The apostles said to the Lord, 'Increase our faith'. 5
The Lord replied, 'Were your faith the size of a mustard 6
seed you could say to this mulberry tree, "Be uprooted
and planted in the sea", and it would obey you.

Humble service

'Which of you, with a servant ploughing or minding 7
sheep, would say to him when he returned from the
fields, "Come and have your meal immediately"?
Would he not be more likely to say, "Get my supper 8
laid; make yourself tidy and wait on me while I eat
and drink. You can eat and drink yourself afterwards"?
Must he be grateful to the servant for doing what he 9
was told? ·So with you: when you have done all you 10
have been told to do, say, "We are merely servants: we
have done no more than our duty".'

The ten lepers

Now on the way to Jerusalem he travelled along the 11
border between Samaria and Galilee.ᵃ ·As he entered 12
one of the villages, ten lepers came to meet him. They
stood some way off ·and called to him, 'Jesus! Master! 13
Take pity on us.' ·When he saw them he said, 'Go and 14
show yourselves to the priests'. Now as they were going
away they were cleansed. ·Finding himself cured, one of 15
them turned back praising God at the top of his voice
and threw himself at the feet of Jesus and thanked him. 16
The man was a Samaritan. ·This made Jesus say, 'Were 17
not all ten made clean? The other nine, where are they?

18 It seems that no one has come back to give praise to
19 God, except this foreigner.' ·And he said to the man,
'Stand up and go on your way. Your faith has saved
you.'

The coming of the kingdom of God

20 Asked by the Pharisees when the kingdom of God
was to come, he gave them this answer, 'The coming of
the kingdom of God does not admit of observation
21 and there will be no one to say, "Look here! Look
there!" For, you must know, the kingdom of God is
among you.'

The day of the Son of Man

22 He said to the disciples, 'A time will come when you
will long to see one of the days of the Son of Man and
23 will not see it. ·They will say to you, "Look there!"
or, "Look here!" Make no move; do not set off in
24 pursuit; ·for as the lightning flashing from one part of
heaven lights up the other, so will be the Son of Man
25 when his day comes. ·But first he must suffer grievously
and be rejected by this generation.

26 'As it was in Noah's day, so will it also be in the days
27 of the Son of Man. ·People were eating and drinking,
marrying wives and husbands, right up to the day Noah
went into the ark, and the Flood came and destroyed
28 them all. ·It will be the same as it was in Lot's day:
people were eating and drinking, buying and selling,
29 planting and building, ·but the day Lot left Sodom, God
rained fire and brimstone from heaven and it destroyed
30 them all. ·It will be the same when the day comes for
the Son of Man to be revealed.

17 a. Making for the Jordan valley and Jericho; from there he
goes up to Jerusalem.

'When that day comes, anyone on the housetop, with 31
his possessions in the house, must not come down to
collect them, nor must anyone in the fields turn back
either. ·Remember Lot's wife. ·Anyone who tries to 32,33
preserve his life will lose it; and anyone who loses it will
keep it safe. ·I tell you, on that night two will be in one 34
bed: one will be taken, the other left; ·two women will 35
be grinding corn together: one will be taken, the other
left.' ·The disciples interrupted. 'Where, Lord?' they 37
asked. He said, 'Where the body is, there too will the
vultures gather'.

The unscrupulous judge and the importunate widow

18 Then he told them a parable about the need to 1
pray continually and never lose heart. ·'There 2
was a judge in a certain town' he said 'who had neither
fear of God nor respect for man. ·In the same town 3
there was a widow who kept on coming to him and
saying, "I want justice from you against my enemy!"
For a long time he refused, but at last he said to himself, 4
"Maybe I have neither fear of God nor respect for man,
but since she keeps pestering me I must give this widow 5
her just rights, or she will persist in coming and worry
me to death".'

And the Lord said, 'You notice what the unjust judge 6
has to say? ·Now will not God see justice done to his 7
chosen who cry to him day and night even when he
delays to help them? ·I promise you, he will see justice 8
done to them, and done speedily. But when the Son of
Man comes, will he find any faith on earth?'

The Pharisee and the publican

He spoke the following parable to some people who 9
prided themselves on being virtuous and despised

10 everyone else, ·'Two men went up to the Temple to
11 pray, one a Pharisee, the other a tax collector. ·The
Pharisee stood there and said this prayer to himself,
"I thank you, God, that I am not grasping, unjust,
adulterous like the rest of mankind, and particularly
12 that I am not like this tax collector here. ·I fast twice a
13 week; I pay tithes on all I get." ·The tax collector stood
some distance away, not daring even to raise his eyes
to heaven; but he beat his breast and said, "God, be
14 merciful to me, a sinner". ·This man, I tell you, went
home again at rights with God; the other did not. For
everyone who exalts himself will be humbled, but the
man who humbles himself will be exalted.'

Jesus and the children

15   People even brought little children to him, for him to
touch them; but when the disciples saw this they turned
16 away. ·But Jesus called the children to him and said,
'Let the little children come to me, and do not stop
them; for it is to such as these that the kingdom of God
17 belongs. ·I tell you solemnly, anyone who does not
welcome the kingdom of God like a little child will
never enter it.'

The rich aristocrat

18   A member of one of the leading families put this
question to him, 'Good Master, what have I to do to
19 inherit eternal life?' ·Jesus said to him, 'Why do you
20 call me good? No one is good but God alone. ·You
know the commandments: *You must not commit
adultery; You must not kill; You must not steal; You
must not bring false witness; Honour your father and
21 mother.*' ·He replied, 'I have kept all these from my
22 earliest days till now'. ·And when Jesus heard this he

83

said, 'There is still one thing you lack. Sell all that you
own and distribute the money to the poor, and you will
have treasure in heaven; then come, follow me.' ·But 23
when he heard this he was filled with sadness, for he
was very rich.

The danger of riches

Jesus looked at him and said, 'How hard it is for those 24
who have riches to make their way into the kingdom of
God! ·Yes, it is easier for a camel to pass through the 25
eye of a needle than for a rich man to enter the kingdom
of God.' ·'In that case' said the listeners 'who can be 26
saved?' ·'Things that are impossible for men' he replied 27
'are possible for God.'

The reward of renunciation

Then Peter said, 'What about us? We left all we had 28
to follow you.' ·He said to them, 'I tell you solemnly, 29
there is no one who has left house, wife, brothers,
parents or children for the sake of the kingdom of God
who will not be given repayment many times over in 30
this present time and, in the world to come, eternal life'.

Third prophecy of the Passion

· Then taking the Twelve aside he said to them, 'Now 31
we are going up to Jerusalem, and everything that is
written by the prophets about the Son of Man is to
come true. ·For he will be handed over to the pagans 32
and will be mocked, maltreated and spat on, ·and when 33
they have scourged him they will put him to death; and
on the third day he will rise again.' ·But they could 34
make nothing of this; what he said was quite obscure
to them, they had no idea what it meant.

Entering Jericho: the blind man

35 Now as he drew near to Jericho there was a blind man
36 sitting at the side of the road begging. ·When he heard
37 the crowd going past he asked what it was all about, ·and
they told him that Jesus the Nazarene was passing by.
38 So he called out, 'Jesus, Son of David, have pity on
39 me'. ·The people in front scolded him and told him to
keep quiet, but he shouted all the louder, 'Son of David,
40 have pity on me'. ·Jesus stopped and ordered them to
bring the man to him, and when he came up, asked him,
41 'What do you want me to do for you?' 'Sir,' he replied
42 'let me see again.' ·Jesus said to him, 'Receive your
sight. Your faith has saved you.' And instantly his sight
returned and he followed him praising God, and all the
people who saw it gave praise to God for what had
happened.

Zacchaeus

1 **19** He entered Jericho and was going through the
2 town ·when a man whose name was Zacchaeus
made his appearance; he was one of the senior tax
3 collectors and a wealthy man. ·He was anxious to see
what kind of man Jesus was, but he was too short and
4 could not see him from the crowd; ·so he ran ahead
and climbed a sycamore tree to catch a glimpse of Jesus
5 who was to pass that way. ·When Jesus reached the
spot he looked up and spoke to him: 'Zacchaeus, come
down. Hurry, because I must stay at your house today.'
6 And he hurried down and welcomed him joyfully.
7 They all complained when they saw what was happening. 'He has gone to stay at a sinner's house, they said.
8 But Zacchaeus stood his ground and said to the Lord,
'Look, sir, I am going to give half my property to the

poor, and if I have cheated anybody I will pay him back four times the amount'.[a] ·And Jesus said to him, 'Today 9 salvation has come to this house, because this man too is a son of Abraham;[b] ·for the Son of Man has come to 10 seek out and save what was lost'.

Parable of the pounds

While the people were listening to this he went on to 11 tell a parable, because he was near Jerusalem and they imagined that the kingdom of God was going to show itself then and there. ·Accordingly he said, 'A man of 12 noble birth went to a distant country to be appointed king and afterwards return.[c] ·He summoned ten of his 13 servants and gave them ten pounds. "Do business with these" he told them "until I get back." ·But his com- 14 patriots detested him and sent a delegation to follow him with this message, "We do not want this man to be our king".

'Now on his return, having received his appointment 15 as king, he sent for those servants to whom he had given the money, to find out what profit each had made. ·The 16 first came in and said, "Sir, your one pound has brought in ten". ·"Well done, my good servant!" he replied 17 "Since you have proved yourself faithful in a very small thing, you shall have the government of ten cities." Then came the second and said, "Sir, your one pound 18 has made five". ·To this one also he said, "And you shall 19 be in charge of five cities". ·Next came the other and 20 said, "Sir, here is your pound. I put it away safely in a piece of linen ·because I was afraid of you; for you are 21 an exacting man: you pick up what you have not put down and reap what you have not sown." ·"You wicked 22 servant!" he said "Out of your own mouth I condemn you. So you knew I was an exacting man, picking up

what I have not put down and reaping what I have not
23 sown? ·Then why did you not put my money in the
bank? On my return I could have drawn it out with
24 interest." ·And he said to those standing by, "Take the
pound from him and give it to the man who has ten
25 pounds". ·And they said to him, "But, sir, he has ten
26 pounds . . ." ·"I tell you, to everyone who has will be
given more; but from the man who has not, even what
he has will be taken away.

27   "But as for my enemies who did not want me for
their king, bring them here and execute them in my
presence." '

V. THE JERUSALEM MINISTRY

The Messiah enters Jerusalem

28   When he had said this he went on ahead, going up to
29 Jerusalem. ·Now when he was near Bethphage and
Bethany, close by the Mount of Olives as it is called, he
30 sent two of the disciples, telling them, ·'Go off to the
village opposite, and as you enter it you will find a
tethered colt that no one has yet ridden. Untie it and
31 bring it here. ·If anyone asks you, "Why are you untying
32 it?" you are to say this, "The Master needs it".' ·The
messengers went off and found everything just as he had
33 told them. ·As they were untying the colt, its owner

19 a. I.e. at the highest rate known to Jewish law (Ex 21:37) or the
rate imposed by Roman law on convicted thieves.
b. Although he belongs to a profession generally ranked with
pagans.
c. Probably alluding to the journey of Archelaus to Rome in
4 B.C. to have the will of Herod the Great confirmed in his
favour. A deputation of Jews followed him there to contest his
claim.

said, 'Why are you untying that colt?' •and they 34
answered, 'The Master needs it'.

So they took the colt to Jesus, and throwing their 35
garments over its back they helped Jesus on to it. •As 36
he moved off, people spread their cloaks in the road,
and now, as he was approaching the downward slope 37
of the Mount of Olives, the whole group of disciples
joyfully began to praise God at the top of their voices
for all the miracles they had seen. •They cried out: 38

> '*Blessings on the King who comes,*
> *in the name of the Lord!*
> Peace in heaven
> and glory in the highest heavens!'

Jesus defends his disciples for acclaiming him

Some Pharisees in the crowd said to him, 'Master, 39
check your disciples', •but he answered, 'I tell you, if 40
these keep silence the stones will cry out'.

Lament for Jerusalem

As he drew near and came in sight of the city he shed 41
tears over it •and said, 'If you in your turn had only 42
understood on this day the message of peace! But,
alas, it is hidden from your eyes! •Yes, a time is coming 43
when your enemies will raise fortifications all round
you, when they will encircle you and hem you in on
every side; •they will dash you and the children inside 44
your walls to the ground; they will leave not one stone
standing on another within you—and all because you
did not recognise your opportunity when God offered
it!'

The expulsion of the dealers from the Temple

Then he went into the Temple and began driving out 45

46 those who were selling. ·'According to scripture,' he said *my house will be a house of prayer*.[d] But you have turned it into *a robbers' den*.'[e]

Jesus teaches in the Temple

47 He taught in the Temple every day. The chief priests and the scribes, with the support of the leading citizens,
48 tried to do away with him, ·but they did not see how they could carry this out because the people as a whole hung on his words.

The Jews question the authority of Jesus

1 **20** Now one day while he was teaching the people in the Temple and proclaiming the Good News, the chief priests and the scribes came up, together
2 with the elders, ·and spoke to him. 'Tell us' they said 'what authority have you for acting like this? Or who
3 is it that gave you this authority?' ·'And I' replied
4 Jesus 'will ask you a question. Tell me: ·John's baptism:
5 did it come from heaven, or from man?' ·And they argued it out this way among themselves, 'If we say from heaven, he will say, "Why did you refuse to
6 believe him?"; ·and if we say from man, the people will all stone us, for they are convinced that John was a
7 prophet'. ·So their reply was that they did not know
8 where it came from. ·And Jesus said to them, 'Nor will I tell you my authority for acting like this'.

Parable of the wicked husbandmen

9 And he went on to tell the people this parable: 'A man planted a vineyard and leased it to tenants, and
10 went abroad for a long while. ·When the time came, he

d. Is 56:7.   **e.** Jr 7:11.

sent a servant to the tenants to get his share of the
produce of the vineyard from them. But the tenants
thrashed him, and sent him away empty-handed. ·But 11
he persevered and sent a second servant; they thrashed
him too and treated him shamefully and sent him away
empty-handed. ·He still persevered and sent a third; 12
they wounded this one also, and threw him out. ·Then 13
the owner of the vineyard said, "What am I to do? I will
send them my dear son. Perhaps they will respect him."
But when the tenants saw him they put their heads 14
together. "This is the heir," they said "let us kill him so
that the inheritance will be ours." ·So they threw him 15
out of the vineyard and killed him.

'Now what will the owner of the vineyard do to them?
He will come and make an end of these tenants and 16
give the vineyard to others.' Hearing this they said,
'God forbid!' ·But he looked hard at them and said, 17
'Then what does this text in the scriptures mean:

> *It was the stone rejected by the builders*
> *that became the keystone?[a]*

Anyone who falls on that stone will be dashed to 18
pieces; anyone it falls on will be crushed.'

But for their fear of the people, the scribes and the 19
chief priests would have liked to lay hands on him that
very moment, because they realised that this parable
was aimed at them.

On tribute to Caesar

So they waited their opportunity and sent agents to 20
pose as men devoted to the Law, and to fasten on something he might say and so enable them to hand him over
to the jurisdiction and authority of the governor. ·They 21
put to him this question, 'Master, we know that you

say and teach what is right; you favour no one, but
22 teach the way of God in all honesty. ·Is it permissible
23 for us to pay taxes to Caesar or not?' ·But he was aware
24 of their cunning and said, ·'Show me a denarius. Whose
25 head and name are on it?' 'Caesar's' they said. ·'Well
then,' he said to them 'give back to Caesar what belongs
to Caesar—and to God what belongs to God.'

26 As a result, they were unable to find fault with
anything he had to say in public; his answer took them
by surprise and they were silenced.

The resurrection of the dead

27 Some Sadducees—those who say that there is no
resurrection—approached him and they put this question
28 to him, ·'Master, we have it from Moses in writing,
that if a man's married brother dies childless, the man
must marry the widow to raise up children for his
29 brother. ·Well then, there were seven brothers. The
30 first, having married a wife, died childless. ·The second
31 and then the third married the widow. And the same
32 with all seven, they died leaving no children. ·Finally
33 the woman herself died. ·Now, at the resurrection, to
which of them will she be wife since she had been
married to all seven?'

34 Jesus replied, 'The children of this world take wives
35 and husbands, ·but those who are judged worthy of a
place in the other world and in the resurrection from the
36 dead do not marry ·because they can no longer die, for
they are the same as the angels, and being children of
37 the resurrection they are sons of God. ·And Moses himself implies that the dead rise again, in the passage about
the bush where he calls the Lord *the God of Abraham,*

20 a. Ps 118:22.

91

the God of Isaac and the God of Jacob.[b] ·Now he is God, 38
not of the dead, but of the living; for to him all men
are in fact alive.'

Some scribes[c] then spoke up. 'Well put, Master' they 39
said ·—because they would not dare to ask him any 40
more questions.

Christ, not only son but also Lord of David

He then said to them, 'How can people maintain that 41
the Christ is son of David? ·Why, David himself says 42
in the Book of Psalms:

> *The Lord said to my Lord:*
> *Sit at my right hand*
> *and I will make your enemies* 43
> *a footstool for you.*[d]

David here calls him Lord; how then can he be his son?' 44

The scribes condemned by Jesus

While all the people were listening he said to the 45
disciples, ·'Beware of the scribes who like to walk about 46
in long robes and love to be greeted obsequiously in the
market squares, to take the front seats in the synagogues
and the places of honour at banquets, ·who swallow 47
the property of widows, while making a show of lengthy
prayers. The more severe will be the sentence they
receive.'

The widow's mite

21 As he looked up he saw rich people putting their 1
offerings into the treasury; ·then he happened to 2
notice a poverty-stricken widow putting in two small
coins, ·and he said, 'I tell you truly, this poor widow has 3
put in more than any of them; ·for these have all con- 4

tributed money they had over, but she from the little
she had has put in all she had to live on'.

Discourse on the destruction of Jerusalem:[a] Introduction

5 When some were talking about the Temple, remarking
how it was adorned with fine stonework and votive
6 offerings, he said, ·'All these things you are staring at
now—the time will come when not a single stone will be
7 left on another: everything will be destroyed'. ·And they
put to him this question: 'Master,' they said 'when will
this happen, then, and what sign will there be that this is
about to take place?'

The warning signs

8 'Take care not to be deceived,' he said 'because many
will come using my name and saying, "I am he" and,
9 "The time is near at hand". Refuse to join them. ·And
when you hear of wars and revolutions, do not be
frightened, for this is something that must happen but
10 the end is not so soon.' ·Then he said to them, 'Nation
will fight against nation, and kingdom against kingdom.
11 There will be great earthquakes and plagues and
famines here and there; there will be fearful sights and
great signs from heaven.
12 'But before all this happens, men will seize you and
persecute you; they will hand you over to the synagogues and to imprisonment, and bring you before
13 kings and governors because of my name·—and that

b. Ex 3:6.
c. Most scribes were Pharisees and believed in the resurrection of
the dead.
d. Ps 110:1.
21 a. This passage on the End Time also includes some elements of
a prophecy of the destruction of Jerusalem.

will be your opportunity to bear witness. ·Keep this 14
carefully in mind: you are not to prepare your defence,
because I myself shall give you an eloquence and a wis- 15
dom that none of your opponents will be able to resist
or contradict. ·You will be betrayed even by parents 16
and brothers, relations and friends; and some of you
will be put to death. ·You will be hated by all men on 17
account of my name, ·but not a hair of your head will be 18
lost. ·Your endurance will win you your lives.   19

The siege

'When you see Jerusalem surrounded by armies, you 20
must realise that she will soon be laid desolate. ·Then 21
those in Judaea must escape to the mountains, those
inside the city must leave it, and those in country districts
must not take refuge in it. ·For this is the time of 22
vengeance when all that scripture says*b* must be fulfilled. ·Alas for those with child, or with babies at the 23
breast, when those days come!

The disaster and the age of the pagans

'For great misery will descend on the land and wrath
on this people. ·They will fall by the edge of the sword 24
and be led captive to every pagan country; and Jerusalem
will be trampled down by the pagans until the age of
the pagans is completely over.

Cosmic disasters and the coming of the Son of Man

'There will be signs in the sun and moon and stars; 25
on earth nations in agony, bewildered by the clamour of
the ocean and its waves; ·men dying of fear as they 26
await what menaces the world, for the powers of heaven
will be shaken. ·And then they will see the Son of Man 27
coming in a cloud with power and great glory. ·When 28

these things begin to take place, stand erect, hold your heads high, because your liberation^c is near at hand.'

The time of this coming

29 And he told them a parable, 'Think of the fig tree
30 and indeed every tree. ·As soon as you see them bud,
31 you know that summer is now near. ·So with you when you see these things happening: know that the kingdom
32 of God is near. ·I tell you solemnly, before this generation
33 has passed away all will have taken place. ·Heaven and earth will pass away, but my words will never pass away.

Be on the alert

34 'Watch yourselves, or your hearts will be coarsened with debauchery and drunkenness and the cares of life, and that day will be sprung on you suddenly, like a trap.
35 For it will come down on every living man on the face
36 of the earth. ·Stay awake, praying at all times for the strength to survive all that is going to happen, and to stand with confidence before the Son of Man.'

The last days of Jesus

37 In the daytime he would be in the Temple teaching, but would spend the night on the hill called the Mount
38 of Olives. ·And from early morning the people would gather round him in the Temple to listen to him.

VI. THE PASSION

The conspiracy against Jesus: Judas betrays him

1
2 **22** The feast of Unleavened Bread, called the Passover, was now drawing near, ·and the chief priests and the scribes were looking for some way of

b. Possibly alluding to Dn 9:27.   **c.** Or 'redemption'.

doing away with him, because they mistrusted the people.

Then Satan entered into Judas, surnamed Iscariot, 3 who was numbered among the Twelve. ·He went to the 4 chief priests and the officers of the guard^a to discuss a scheme for handing Jesus over to them. ·They were 5 delighted and agreed to give him money. ·He accepted, 6 and looked for an opportunity to betray him to them without the people knowing.

Preparation for the Passover supper

The day of Unleavened Bread came round, the day 7 on which the passover had to be sacrificed, ·and he sent 8 Peter and John, saying, 'Go and make the preparations for us to eat the passover'. ·'Where do you want us to 9 prepare it?' they asked. ·'Listen,' he said 'as you go into 10 the city you will meet a man carrying a pitcher of water. Follow him into the house he enters ·and tell the owner 11 of the house, "The Master has this to say to you: Where is the dining room in which I can eat the passover with my disciples?" ·The man will show you a large upper 12 room furnished with couches. Make the preparations there.' ·They set off and found everything as he had told 13 them, and prepared the Passover.

The supper

When the hour came he took his place at table, and 14 the apostles with him. ·And he said to them, 'I have 15 longed to eat this passover with you before I suffer; because, I tell you, I shall not eat it again until it is 16 fulfilled in the kingdom of God'.

Then, taking a cup,^b he gave thanks and said, 'Take 17 this and share it among you, ·because from now on, I 18 tell you, I shall not drink wine until the kingdom of God comes'.

The institution of the Eucharist

19 Then he took some bread, and when he had given thanks, broke it and gave it to them saying, 'This is my body which will be given for you; do this as a
20 memorial of me'. ·He did the same with the cup after supper, and said, 'This cup is the new covenant in my blood which will be poured out for you.

The treachery of Judas foretold

21 'And yet, here with me on the table is the hand of the
22 man who betrays me. ·The Son of Man does indeed go to his fate even as it has been decreed, but alas for that
23 man by whom he is betrayed!' ·And they began to ask one another which of them it could be who was to do this thing.

Who is the greatest?

24 A dispute arose also between them about which
25 should be reckoned the greatest, ·but he said to them, 'Among pagans it is the kings who lord it over them, and those who have authority over them are given the
26 title Benefactor. ·This must not happen with you. No; the greatest among you must behave as if he were the youngest, the leader as if he were the one who serves.
27 For who is the greater: the one at table or the one who serves? The one at table, surely? Yet here am I among you as one who serves!

22 a. The Temple police, chosen from among the Levites.
b. Luke distinguishes the Passover and the cup of vv. 15–18 from the bread and the cup of vv. 19–20.

The reward promised to the apostles

'You are the men who have stood by me faithfully in 28
my trials; ·and now I confer a kingdom on you, just as 29
my Father conferred one on me: ·you will eat and drink 30
at my table in my kingdom, and you will sit on thrones
to judge the twelve tribes of Israel.

Peter's denial and repentance foretold

'Simon, Simon! Satan, you must know, has got his 31
wish to sift you all like wheat; ·but I have prayed for 32
you, Simon, that your faith may not fail, and once you
have recovered, you in your turn must strengthen your
brothers.' ·'Lord,' he answered 'I would be ready to go 33
to prison with you, and to death.' ·Jesus replied, 'I tell 34
you, Peter, by the time the cock crows today you will
have denied three times that you know me'.

A time of crisis

He said to them, 'When I sent you out without purse 35
or haversack or sandals, were you short of anything?
'No' they said. He said to them, 'But now if you have a 36
purse, take it; if you have a haversack, do the same; if
you have no sword, sell your cloak and buy one,
because I tell you these words of scripture have to be 37
fulfilled in me: *He let himself be taken for a criminal.*ᶜ
Yes, what scripture says about me is even now reaching
its fulfilment.' ·'Lord,' they said 'there are two swords 38
here now.' He said to them, 'That is enough!'

The Mount of Olives

He then left to make his way as usual to the Mount of 39
Olives, with the disciples following. ·When they reached 40
the place he said to them, 'Pray not to be put to the
test'.

41 Then he withdrew from them, about a stone's throw
42 away, and knelt down and prayed. ·'Father,' he said 'if
you are willing, take this cup away from me. Neverthe-
43 less, let your will be done, not mine.' ·Then an angel
appeared to him, coming from heaven to give him
44 strength. ·In his anguish he prayed even more earnestly,
and his sweat fell to the ground like drops of blood.
45 When he rose from prayer he went to the disciples
46 and found them sleeping for sheer grief. ·'Why are you
asleep?' he said to them. 'Get up and pray not to be put
to the test.'

The arrest

47 He was still speaking when a number of men
appeared, and at the head of them the man called Judas,
one of the Twelve, who went up to Jesus to kiss him.
48 Jesus said, 'Judas, are you betraying the Son of Man
49 with a kiss?' ·His followers, seeing what was happening,
50 said, 'Lord, shall we use our swords?' ·And one of them
struck out at the high priest's servant, and cut off his
51 right ear. ·But at this Jesus spoke. 'Leave off!' he said
'That will do!' And touching the man's ear he healed
him.
52 Then Jesus spoke to the chief priests and captains of
the Temple guard and elders who had come for him.
'Am I a brigand' he said 'that you had to set out with
53 swords and clubs? ·When I was among you in the Temple
day after day you never moved to lay hands on me.
But this is your hour; this is the reign of darkness.'

Peter's denials

54 They seized him then and led him away, and they took
him to the high priest's house. Peter followed at a

c. Is 53:12.

99

distance. ·They had lit a fire in the middle of the court- 55
yard and Peter sat down among them, ·and as he was 56
sitting there by the blaze a servant-girl saw him, peered
at him, and said, 'This person was with him too'. ·But 57
he denied it. 'Woman,' he said 'I do not know him.'
Shortly afterwards someone else saw him and said, 58
'You are another of them'. But Peter replied, 'I am not,
my friend'. ·About an hour later another man insisted, 59
saying, 'This fellow was certainly with him. Why, he is
a Galilean.' ·'My friend,' said Peter 'I do not know 60
what you are talking about.' At that instant, while he
was still speaking, the cock crew, ·and the Lord turned 61
and looked straight at Peter, and Peter remembered
what the Lord had said to him, 'Before the cock crows
today, you will have disowned me three times'. ·And 62
he went outside and wept bitterly.

Jesus mocked by the guards

Meanwhile the men who guarded Jesus were mocking 63
and beating him. ·They blindfolded him and questioned 64
him. 'Play the prophet' they said. 'Who hit you then?'
And they continued heaping insults on him. 65

Jesus before the Sanhedrin

When day broke there was a meeting of the elders of 66
the people, attended by the chief priests and scribes.
He was brought before their council, ·and they said to 67
him, 'If you are the Christ, tell us'. 'If I tell you,' he
replied 'you will not believe me, ·and if I question you, 68
you will not answer. ·But from now on, the Son of Man 69
will be *seated at the right hand* of the Power *of God.*'*d*
Then they all said, 'So you are the Son of God then?' 70
He answered, 'It is you who say I am'. ·'What need of 71
witnesses have we now?' they said. 'We have heard it for

1 ourselves from his own lips.' **23** The whole assembly
then rose, and they brought him before Pilate.

Jesus before Pilate

2 They began their accusation by saying, 'We found
this man inciting our people to revolt, opposing pay-
ment of the tribute to Caesar, and claiming to be Christ,
3 a king'. ·Pilate put to him this question, 'Are you the
king of the Jews?' 'It is you who say it' he replied.
4 Pilate then said to the chief priests and the crowd, 'I
5 find no case against this man'. ·But they persisted, 'He is
inflaming the people with his teaching all over Judaea; it
has come all the way from Galilee, where he started,
6 down to here'. ·When Pilate heard this, he asked if the
7 man were a Galilean; ·and finding that he came under
Herod's jurisdiction he passed him over to Herod who
was also in Jerusalem at that time.

Jesus before Herod

8 Herod was delighted to see Jesus; he had heard about
him and had been wanting for a long time to set eyes on
him; moreover, he was hoping to see some miracle
9 worked by him. ·So he questioned him at some length;
10 but without getting any reply. ·Meanwhile the chief
priests and the scribes were there, violently pressing
11 their accusations. ·Then Herod, together with his
guards, treated him with contempt and made fun of
him; he put a rich cloak[a] on him and sent him back to
12 Pilate. ·And though Herod and Pilate had been enemies
before, they were reconciled that same day.

Jesus before Pilate again

13 Pilate then summoned the chief priests and the

d. Ps 110:1.   **23 a.** Ceremonial dress of a prince.

101

leading men and the people. ·'You brought this man 14
before me' he said 'as a political agitator. Now I have
gone into the matter myself in your presence and found
no case against the man in respect of all the charges you
bring against him. ·Nor has Herod either, since he has 15
sent him back to us. As you can see, the man has done
nothing that deserves death, ·so I shall have him flogged 16
and then let him go.' ·But as one man they howled, 18
'Away with him! Give us Barabbas!' ·(This man had 19
been thrown into prison for causing a riot in the city
and for murder.)

Pilate was anxious to set Jesus free and addressed 20
them again, ·but they shouted back, 'Crucify him! 21
Crucify him!' ·And for the third time he spoke to them, 22
'Why? What harm has this man done? I have found no
case against him that deserves death, so I shall have
him punished and then let him go.' ·But they kept on 23
shouting at the top of their voices, demanding that he
should be crucified. And their shouts were growing
louder.

Pilate then gave his verdict: their demand was to be 24
granted. ·He released the man they asked for, who had 25
been imprisoned for rioting and murder, and handed
Jesus over to them to deal with as they pleased.

The way to Calvary

As they were leading him away they seized on a man, 26
Simon from Cyrene, who was coming in from the
country, and made him shoulder the cross and carry it
behind Jesus. ·Large numbers of people followed him, 27
and of women too,[b] who mourned and lamented for
him. ·But Jesus turned to them and said, 'Daughters of 28
Jerusalem, do not weep for me; weep rather for yourselves and for your children. ·For the days will surely 29

come when people will say, "Happy are those who are
barren, the wombs that have never borne, the breasts
30 that have never suckled!" ·Then they will begin to *say to
the mountains, "Fall on us!"; to the hills, "Cover us!"*ᶜ
31 For if men use the green wood like this, what will
32 happen when it is dry?' ·Now with him they were also
leading out two other criminals to be executed.

The crucifixion

33 When they reached the place called The Skull, they
crucified him there and the two criminals also, one on
34 the right, the other on the left. ·Jesus said, 'Father,
forgive them; they do not know what they are doing'.
Then they cast lots to share out his clothing.

The crucified Christ is mocked

35 The people stayed there watching him. As for the
leaders, they jeered at him. 'He saved others,' they said
'let him save himself if he is the Christ of God, the
36 Chosen One.' ·The soldiers mocked him too, and when
37 they approached to offer him vinegar ·they said, 'If
38 you are the king of the Jews, save yourself'. ·Above him
there was an inscription: 'This is the King of the Jews'.

The good thief

39 One of the criminals hanging there abused him. 'Are
you not the Christ?' he said. 'Save yourself and us as
40 well.' ·But the other spoke up and rebuked him. 'Have
you no fear of God at all?' he said. 'You got the same
41 sentence as he did, ·but in our case we deserved it: we

b. The Talmud records that noblewomen of Jerusalem used to
give soothing drinks to condemned criminals.
c. Ho 10:8.

are paying for what we did. But this man has done
nothing wrong. ·Jesus,' he said 'remember me when 42
you come into your kingdom.' ·'Indeed, I promise you,' 43
he replied 'today you will be with me in paradise.'

The death of Jesus

It was now about the sixth hour and, with the sun 44
eclipsed, a darkness came over the whole land until the
ninth hour. ·The veil of the Temple was torn right down 45
the middle; ·and when Jesus had cried out in a loud 46
voice, he said, 'Father, *into your hands I commit my
spirit*'.*a* With these words he breathed his last.

After the death

When the centurion saw what had taken place, he 47
gave praise to God and said, 'This was a great and good
man'. ·And when all the people who had gathered for 48
the spectacle saw what had happened, they went home
beating their breasts.

All his friends stood at a distance; so also did the 49
women who had accompanied him from Galilee, and
they saw all this happen.

The burial

Then a member of the council arrived, an upright 50
and virtuous man named Joseph. ·He had not consented 51
to what the others had planned and carried out. He
came from Arimathaea, a Jewish town, and he lived in
the hope of seeing the kingdom of God. ·This man went 52
to Pilate and asked for the body of Jesus. ·He then took 53
it down, wrapped it in a shroud and put him in a tomb
which was hewn in stone in which no one had yet been
laid. ·It was Preparation Day and the sabbath was 54
imminent.

55   Meanwhile the women who had come from Galilee
with Jesus were following behind. They took note of the
tomb and of the position of the body.

56   Then they returned and prepared spices and oint-
ments. And on the sabbath day they rested, as the Law
required.

VII. AFTER THE RESURRECTION

The empty tomb. The angel's message

1 **24** On the first day of the week, at the first sign of
dawn, they went to the tomb with the spices they
2 had prepared. ·They found that the stone had been
3 rolled away from the tomb, ·but on entering discovered
4 that the body of the Lord Jesus was not there. ·As they
stood there not knowing what to think, two men in
brilliant clothes suddenly appeared at their side.
5 Terrified, the women lowered their eyes. But the two
men said to them, 'Why look among the dead for
6 someone who is alive? ·He is not here; he has risen.
Remember what he told you when he was still in
7 Galilee: ·that the Son of Man had to be handed over
into the power of sinful men and be crucified, and rise
8 again on the third day.' ·And they remembered his
words.

The apostles refuse to believe the women

9   When the women returned from the tomb they told
10 all this to the Eleven and to all the others. ·The women
were Mary of Magdala, Joanna, and Mary the mother
of James. The other women with them also told the

d. Ps 31:5.

apostles, ·but this story of theirs seemed pure nonsense, 11
and they did not believe them.

Peter at the tomb

Peter, however, went running to the tomb, He bent 12
down and saw the binding cloths but nothing else; he
then went back home, amazed at what had happened.

The road to Emmaus

That very same day, two of them were on their way 13
to a village called Emmaus, seven miles*a* from
Jerusalem, ·and they were talking together about all 14
that had happened. ·Now as they talked this over, 15
Jesus himself came up and walked by their side; ·but 16
something prevented them from recognising him. ·He 17
said to them, 'What matters are you discussing as you
walk along?' They stopped short, their faces downcast.

Then one of them, called Cleopas, answered him, 18
'You must be the only person staying in Jerusalem who
does not know the things that have been happening
there these last few days'. ·'What things?' he asked. 'All 19
about Jesus of Nazareth' they answered 'who proved he
was a great prophet by the things he said and did in the
sight of God and of the whole people; ·and how our 20
chief priests and our leaders handed him over to be
sentenced to death, and had him crucified. ·Our own 21
hope had been that he would be the one to set Israel
free. And this is not all: two whole days have gone by
since it all happened; ·and some women from our group 22
have astounded us: they went to the tomb in the early
morning, ·and when they did not find the body, they 23
came back to tell us they had seen a vision of angels who
declared he was alive. ·Some of our friends went to the 24

tomb and found everything exactly as the women had reported, but of him they saw nothing.'

25 Then he said to them, 'You foolish men! So slow to
26 believe the full message of the prophets! ·Was it not ordained that the Christ should suffer and so enter
27 into his glory?' ·Then, starting with Moses and going through all the prophets, he explained to them the passages throughout the scriptures that were about himself.

28 When they drew near to the village to which they
29 were going, he made as if to go on; ·but they pressed him to stay with them. 'It is nearly evening' they said 'and the day is almost over.' So he went in to stay with
30 them. ·Now while he was with them at table, he took the bread and said the blessing; then he broke it and handed
31 it to them. ·And their eyes were opened and they recognised him; but he had vanished from their sight.
32 Then they said to each other, 'Did not our hearts burn within us as he talked to us on the road and explained the scriptures to us?'

33 They set out that instant and returned to Jerusalem. There they found the Eleven assembled together with
34 their companions, ·who said to them, 'Yes, it is true.
35 The Lord has risen and has appeared to Simon.' ·Then they told their story of what had happened on the road and how they had recognised him at the breaking of bread.

Jesus appears to the apostles

36 They were still talking about all this when he himself stood among them and said to them, 'Peace be with
37 you!' ·In a state of alarm and fright, they thought they

24 a. The identity of the village is disputed.

were seeing a ghost. ·But he said, 'Why are you so 38
agitated, and why are these doubts rising in your hearts?
Look at my hands and feet; yes, it is I indeed. Touch 39
me and see for yourselves; a ghost has no flesh and
bones as you can see I have.' ·And as he said this he 40
showed them his hands and feet. ·Their joy was so great 41
that they still could not believe it, and they stood there
dumbfounded; so he said to them, 'Have you anything
here to eat?' ·And they offered him a piece of grilled 42
fish, ·which he took and ate before their eyes. 43

Last instructions to the apostles

Then he told them, 'This is what I meant when I said, 44
while I was still with you, that everything written about
me in the Law of Moses, in the Prophets and in the
Psalms, has to be fulfilled'. ·He then opened their 45
minds to understand the scriptures, ·and he said to 46
them, 'So you see how it is written that the Christ would
suffer and on the third day rise from the dead, ·and 47
that, in his name, repentance for the forgiveness of sins
would be preached to all the nations, beginning from
Jerusalem. ·You are witnesses to this. 48

'And now I am sending down to you what the Father 49
has promised. Stay in the city then, until you are
    clothed with the power from on high.'

The ascension

Then he took them out as far as the outskirts of 50
Bethany, and lifting up his hands he blessed them.
Now as he blessed them, he withdrew from them and 51
was carried up to heaven. ·They worshipped him and 52
then went back to Jerusalem full of joy; ·and they were 53
continually in the Temple praising God.

NOTES

NOTES

1 Prologue

In the first century, authors had to consider the length of the papyrus scrolls available when they planned their work. If it was long and more than one scroll was required, the separate parts were linked by means of prologues which showed the connection of subject matter. Lk used the customary method. See Acts 1:1–5 where reference is made to 'the earlier work', the gospel.

1:1. *Many others.* Perhaps rather an exaggeration. Mark and Q are the only written sources that can be suggested but Q may not have been a single document and it cannot be said that others did not exist. Possibly Lk 1:5–2:52 are based on Aramaic documents.

2. *Exactly as these were handed down . . .* The reference is to the period of oral transmission (Intro E). The importance of accuracy was hammered home by Jewish religious teachers, and the smallest mistakes were regarded as sins. There is no reason to suppose that standards were relaxed when people passed on stories about Jesus.

Eyewitnesses. Lk was dealing with matters of fact and he placed great stress on witness. The primary duty of the apostles was to witness to the fact of the resurrection (Lk 24:48, Acts 1:8, 22; 10:39–40), St Paul was equally decided (I Corinthians 15:3–8),

3. *I in my turn.* Lk was with St Paul during his imprisonment in Jerusalem and Caesarea (Acts 21:17f.) and had ample opportunity for research. It may have been

111

then (A.D. 58–60?) that he collected the material unique to his gospel.

The whole story from the beginning. From the prophecy of the birth of John the Baptist, the Forerunner, and the birth of Jesus to the arrival of the gospel in Rome at the end of Acts.

Theophilus. It is not known who he was, but the title suggests that he was a person of importance. He is also mentioned in Acts 1:1. He may have been a Christian or just some distinguished official who wanted information.

I: THE BIRTH AND HIDDEN LIFE OF JOHN THE BAPTIST AND OF JESUS

Whereas the prologue is written in good Greek, the style and vocabulary of this section suggest that Lk was using Aramaic sources or deliberately writing in an Aramaic style. The birth and infancy stories in St Matthew are told from Joseph's point of view; here they are told from Mary's.

The birth of John the Baptist foretold

1:5. *In the days of King Herod.* Herod the Great (Intro B). Mt 2:1 makes the same statement. Both evangelists were concerned to make clear that what took place was a matter of verifiable history. See also Lk 2:1; 3:1 where the point is further stressed. Herod the Great died in 4 B.C. and Jesus may have been born in 8–6 B.C. The 'Christian Era', established in the 6th century, is the result of a false calculation.

Zechariah and Elizabeth. The elderly pair represent all that was best in Judaism. There was no more exalted office than that of the priests who served in the Temple, the House of the Lord. Lk began here because he wanted to show that Christianity sprang from the highest type of Judaism and far surpassed it. *The Abijah section.* The priests, of whom there were many, were divided into sections, each section being responsible for a week's service. The particular duty of Zechariah was to keep the brazier burning that stood on the altar of incense in front of the Holy of Holies, the sanctuary into which only the high priest might go once a year.

1:13. *You must name him John.* The name means 'Yahweh is gracious'. Yahweh is the Hebrew word for the Lord, His personal name. *Your joy and delight.* Joy is the keynote of these chapters as it was to become characteristic of the early Christians, released from the fears of paganism. St Paul places joy next after love in his list of the fruits of the Spirit (Galatians 5:22).

15. *He must drink no wine.* Men and women sometimes took a vow of service to God, and as a sign that they had done so, abstained from wine and did not cut their hair; they were called Nazarites. It was a very ancient form of vow (Numbers 6:1–8).
He will be filled with the Holy Spirit. Like the prophet Jeremiah (Jer 1:4–10), John was set apart even before birth. He was to be the last and greatest of the prophets of Israel. The Holy Spirit was understood as having been active in these events from the outset (1:15, 35, 41, 67; 2:25–26).

17. *With the spirit and power of Elijah.* The quotation is from Malachi (Mal 3:25), a passage which had given rise to the expectation that Elijah would return to prepare for the coming of the Messiah who would establish the reign of God, and bring back to the true religion those Jews who had left it for foreign gods. See I Kings chapters 17–21 for the Elijah stories. Lk like all the members of the early Church set great store by the Old Testament as showing how Christianity was rooted in Judaism.

1:22. *He could not speak.* Zechariah could not give the customary blessing and so the people realised that he had received a vision.

25. *It has pleased him to take away the humiliation.* In earlier times any trial or adversity was regarded as a punishment for sin and therefore a humiliation, and it was an idea still widely held in the time of Christ. To have no son to keep green the memory of the parents was of course a great grief.

The annunciation

27. *A virgin.* Lk, like Mt 1:18–25, makes plain that Mary was a virgin when she conceived her son. Elizabeth's wonderful conception was a sign of the power and mercy of God, pointing forward to one more stupendous. 'Nothing is impossible to God' (v. 37).
Betrothed to Joseph of the House of David. See also Mt 1:18–20. It was believed that the Messiah would be descended from the royal House. Since Joseph was only foster father of Jesus, Jesus was 'of the House of David' in the same kind of way that under English law an adopted son has full legal status as son.

31. *Jesus.* The name is the same as Joshua and means 'Deliverer' (Mt 1:21).

32. *The Lord will give him the throne.* A king is to be born, but no earthly one; his reign will have no end.

38. *Let what you have said be done to me.* Mary accepted her vocation, her call to be used by God for His purpose. Because of the part she played in the world's salvation, the position of women in western civilisation has been distinctive. In the non-Christian world until fairly recently, following the impact of the west, women have very commonly been accorded little respect as individuals.

THE VIRGIN BIRTH

It is a common mistake to think that belief in the virgin birth is the starting point for acceptance of Jesus as Saviour and Son of God; but that is not so. Faith stands or falls on the resurrection. It was on that issue that the first converts were challenged, the apostles proclaiming themselves as witnesses to the fact (Acts 2:32; 3:15; 10:40–43; I Corinthians 15:1–8). The plan of Mark's gospel demonstrates the same point: nothing is related about the birth and infancy of Jesus, and no less than six of its total sixteen chapters are devoted to the last week of the ministry. Once the resurrection is accepted, the miracles of which the virgin birth is one, fall into perspective.

It is important to realise how curious the story is in relation both to the Jewish converts to Christianity who were the first to tell it, and to the pagan converts for whom Luke was particularly writing. The Jews did not regard celibacy as admirable; indeed to marry and have children was a primary duty. If it was tragic for a married woman to be barren, it was even more so for a woman never to marry at all. Unchastity was at least nominally punishable by death. Yet this story apparently originated in the most devout circle in Judaea where people held fast to the Law and loved it. On the other hand, pagans came to Christianity from a permissive society in which virginity was not esteemed. If the story is not true, its origin is difficult to explain. Finally, it must be

remembered that scholars agree that Luke and
Matthew were ignorant of each other's work,
and we have therefore two independent statements
on the matter, one from a Greek and the other
from a Jewish background.

The visitation

1 : 39. *The hill country of Judah.* Mentioned as well in v. 35.
This, as well as the fact that the story opens in Jerusa-
lem, suggests that this material first circulated in
Judaea.

40. *She . . . greeted Elizabeth.* According to tradition,
Mary and Elizabeth were cousins.

41. *The child leapt in her womb.* The mother was filled
with the Holy Spirit, and the unborn child recognising
the one for whose coming he would prepare, already
acted as prophet.

The Magnificat

46. This song, or canticle, has been used in the public
worship of the Church from a very early date, as also
the Benedictus, vv. 68–79, and the Nunc Dimittis, 2:29–
32. Lk may have fitted them into the narrative at
appropriate points, having found them in use by the
Jerusalem Christians. The Magnificat is reminiscent
of Hannah's song, I Samuel 2:1–10, and Mary is here
almost the personification of Israel, rejoicing in the
culmination of her history.

48. *He has looked upon his lowly handmaid.* This is the
first characteristic Old Testament idea in the song.
God comes to the help not of the rich and powerful,
but of the poor and simple. As Mary was poor and
obscure, so were her people.

49. *The Almighty has done great things for me.* The gift
of God was beyond all expectation.

1:55. *According to the promise he made . . . to Abraham . . .*
This is the second important Old Testament idea in
the song. God always remained faithful to the promise
He first gave to Abraham (Genesis 12:1–5; 17:1–7).

The circumcision of John the Baptist

59. *On the eighth day.* Boys were circumcised and named
on the eighth day after birth. Circumcision is still
obligatory amongst the Jews as a sign of their special
relationship with God, their covenant relationship
(Exodus 19:3–8). By this means the boy was enrolled
as one of God's Chosen People. It was a domestic
ceremony.

66. *The hand of the Lord was with him.* i.e. The Lord
protected him.
The Benedictus. (See note on the Magnificat v. 46.)

68. *He has visited his people.* This is Old Testament
language meaning that God has acted in historical
events.

76. *You shall be called Prophet.* Zechariah's hymn of
thanksgiving now turns into prophecy.
You will go before the Lord. i.e. before God.

78. *The rising Sun.* i.e. The Messiah.

The hidden life of John the Baptist

80. *He lived out in the wilderness.* There were communities
of prophets living in the wilderness. They had no
luxuries and spent their time in studying the Scriptures, in prayer, and meditation. John was probably
at one of them.

The birth of Jesus and the visit of the shepherds

2:1. *Caesar Augustus* (30 B.C.–A.D. 14. See Intro A). This
is a second historical note; Herod the Great was
mentioned 1:5.

2. *Quirinius was governor of Syria.* Nothing is known of this man, but he had Palestine under his control because it came within the province of Syria. There was to be a general census of the whole world, the Empire that is to say, with a view to taxation.

2:5. *The town of David called Bethlehem.* It was King David's birthplace. Although Lk and Mt have different stories to tell about the birth and infancy of Jesus, they agree on basic points: (a) Jesus was born of the virgin Mary; (b) his foster father was Joseph; (c) the birth took place at Bethlehem; (d) it happened when Herod was king. See Mt 1 and 2.

  7. *Her firstborn.* In biblical Greek the term does not necessarily imply younger brothers; it simply emphasises the dignity and rights of the child.

10. *I bring you news of great joy* (1:13).

11. *Christ the Lord.* 'Christ' means 'the Anointed One', the translation into Greek of the Hebrew word 'Messiah' (1:17, 27).

The circumcision of Jesus

21. *When the eighth day came* (1:59). The divine Son of God submitted to the Law by which the lives of all Jews were regulated, and was formally admitted to the Jewish religion like anyone else.

Jesus is presented in the Temple

22. *The day came for them to be purified.* The mother had to be purified after childbirth. The boy had to be consecrated to the Lord, and redeemed (bought back from the Lord) by the offering of sacrifice. The offerings made by Joseph and Mary show that they were poor. Lk is careful to note that the parents of Jesus, like the Baptist's, did all that the Law required.

25. *Simeon . . . looked forward to Israel's comforting.* He looked for the coming of the Messiah, and knew that he would see him before he died.

2:27. *Prompted by the Spirit*. Simeon was filled with, taught, and directed by the Holy Spirit (1:15).
The Nunc Dimittis. (See note on the Magnificat 1:46.)

32. *A light to enlighten the pagans*. This was a point which Lk, coming of heathen stock and writing for people of the same kind, loved to dwell on.

The prophecy of Simeon

34. *He is destined for the fall and rising of many* . . . His presence will prove a vital test as men accept or reject him and God's kingdom.

35. *A sword will pierce your own soul*. Simeon knew that Christ must suffer, and Mary on his account.

The prophecy of Anna

36. *There was a prophetess*. Prophecy was a gift bestowed on women as well as men.

38. *The deliverance of Jerusalem*. The Messiah would begin his work of deliverance at Jerusalem. In this gospel great emphasis is placed on Jerusalem as the centre from which salvation will spread.

The hidden life of Jesus at Nazareth

40. *The child grew to maturity* (1:80). The stories of the Baptist and Jesus are parallel.

Jesus among the doctors of the Law

42. *When he was twelve years old*. At twelve a Jewish boy attained his majority and was responsible for keeping the Law: to go to Jerusalem for the Passover was obligatory. Again Lk shows Jesus conforming to the requirement of the Law.

49. *I must be busy with my Father's affairs*. Jesus was the Son of God as well as the son of Mary.

THE INCARNATION

The word 'incarnation' is derived from the Latin and means 'embodiment in flesh'. Jesus was God Incarnate, God in the flesh. Jn 1:1–18 describes Jesus as 'the Word', the expression in human terms of what God is and what God does. 'He was with God in the beginning', there from all eternity. How God could compact himself within the limits of a human person is a mystery beyond the comprehension of the human mind, but believers accept the fact that God is beyond their understanding. Belief in the Incarnation is not the result of reasoning and analysis, but of the recognition of the power of Christ in daily life.

ANGELS

Belief in angels found expression in the later literature of the old Testament, particularly in the book of Daniel where the angel Gabriel is named. As the idea of God surpassing human understanding grew, so it seemed sensible to suppose that He had messengers to send on His errands. The word 'angel' comes from the Greek meaning messenger. Our Lord spoke of them (Lk 20:36) and belief in them is common to all the books of the New Testament, and prominent in Luke–Acts.

II. PRELUDE TO THE PUBLIC MINISTRY OF JESUS

The preaching of John the Baptist (Mt ch. 3)

3:1. *In the fifteenth year of Tiberius Caesar* ... This is Lk's third historical note (1:5; 2:1) (Intro. A). Tiberius having succeeded Augustus in 14, the fifteenth year would be 28 or 29 according to the Roman or Syrian methods of calculation. Jesus was by then at least 33 years old, and possibly more (1:5).

Tetrarch. A Greek word meaning ruler, originally ruler of a fourth part.

3:2. *Annas and Caiaphas.* There was only one high priest in office at a time. Annas was deposed by the Romans in 18, Caiaphas his son-in-law being put in his place and holding office 18–36. Annas may be mentioned here because he was very influential even after his removal. He is also mentioned Jn 18:13, 24.

The word of God came to John. Like the prophets of the Old Testament, the time came when John knew himself to be impelled by God to preach. His hearers recognised this and were profoundly moved. For centuries there had been no prophet and the lack had been accepted as punishment for national sin.

3. *Jordan district.* Probably near Jericho.

A baptism of repentance for the forgiveness of sins. The water of baptism symbolised the complete removal of sin consequent upon repentance. The baptism of John foreshadowed the forgiveness which Jesus would later bestow, and which the Church would in due course proclaim. Forgiveness is a matter of central importance in this gospel.

4. *As it is written.* Isaiah 40:3–5. The conclusion of the quotation is important; salvation is for all mankind (2:32).

7. *The crowds who came* (Mt 3:7; Intro B). There were probably three groups of people in the crowds: (i) Pharisees and Sadducees, the leaders of the people; (ii) The simple country folk; (iii) 'Sinners', tax collectors, soldiers, and people who mixed freely with non-Jews, neglecting the Oral Law.

3:8. *We have Abraham for our father.* The Pharisees and Sadducees made the mistake of thinking that the accident of being born Jews assured them of salvation, regardless of their humility, compassion and justice (Micah 6:8).

9. *The axe is laid to the root of the trees.* Like the Old Testament prophets John taught that the Day of Judgement would precede the establishment of the kingdom of God.

16. *I am not fit to undo the strap of his sandals.* That was the duty of a slave.
He will baptise you with the Holy Spirit and fire. Christ's baptism would have something in addition to the cleansing from sin. Sins must be replaced by positive virtues and for this the help of the Holy Spirit is necessary (Jn 3:1–8). Tongues of fire descended on the apostles at Pentecost (Acts 2:1–13), suggesting the illuminating as well as the cleansing activity of the Holy Spirit.

17. *His winnowing fan is in his hand.* Winnowing is fanning the useless chaff away from grain; in this figure the Messiah is imagined as blowing the sinners away and preserving the faithful.

18. *The Good News.* i.e. The Messiah would come soon; God's reign would begin.

John the Baptist imprisoned

For the story of John's imprisonment and death see Mk 6:14–29. It was not only for personal reasons that Herod feared John. John had a huge following and Herod was afraid that he might head a rebellion. If that happened Herod would be in trouble with the Romans as he was responsible for the good order of Galilee.
Jesus is baptised (Mk 1:9–11; Mt 3:13–17).

3:21. *Jesus . . . was at prayer.* Lk mentions the prayer of Jesus more frequently than Mt or Mk.

Heaven opened. This suggests the directness of communication between Jesus and the Father.

22. *The Holy Spirit . . . in bodily shape like a dove.* Lk accepted literally the tradition as it reached him. Originally the mention of the dove may have been an allusion to the Creation Story (Genesis 1:2) where God's spirit hovered over the water. With the coming of Christ, that is to say, the whole process of creation was given a fresh start.

You are my Son, the Beloved. There are two points to notice about these words. (i) There is a statement about the unique relationship between Jesus and the Father. (ii) The words reflect the thought of a series of poems in Isaiah known as the Servant Songs. The Servant, by his patience under unmerited punishment, and eventual exaltation, presented a challenge to those who looked on, bringing them to repentance and salvation. There seems no doubt that Jesus taught his disciples that it was these passages of Scripture that were prophetic of himself and his work rather than others which refer to the coming of a royal warrior (Isaiah 42:1–9; 49:1–6; 50:4–11; 52:13–53:12).

THE SIGNIFICANCE OF THE BAPTISM OF JESUS

(i) Jesus was always sinless and therefore his baptism was not for the washing away of his sins. On the contrary, it was the occasion when he shouldered the sins of the whole world and began his public work as Messiah.

(ii) We have seen that 'Messiah' and 'Christ' both mean 'Anointed One' (2:11). At his baptism Jesus was anointed with the Holy Spirit ready to begin his public ministry. Both kings and priests were anointed in ancient Israel before entering office. The angel Gabriel had told Mary that the Lord would give her son a throne; thus the anointing at his baptism was as it were the beginning of his kingship. It was the beginning of his priesthood too: the special duty of the priests was to offer sacrifice. Both priest and victim, Jesus offered himself to God on the cross. Both the kingship and the priesthood of the past came to their perfection in the kingship and priesthood of Jesus, and his baptism was the moment of his inauguration.

(iii) The prophets were the third outstanding group of men in ancient Israel and here also we can see Jesus as the fulfilment of all that had gone before. They were mouthpieces of God, telling the people what He was like and what He required of them. Many of them had a tremendous experience of His presence before their ministries began, and the baptism was a similar experience (Amos 7:15; Isaiah 6:1–7).

The ancestry of Jesus

3:23. Both this genealogy and that in Mt 1:1–16 are artificial constructions used as a method of making certain statements about Jesus. Lk detailed his human ancestry to contrast with the divine relationship indicated in v. 22, and the line is traced back to Adam to show Christ's kinship with all mankind. Mt on the other hand begins with Abraham and remains within the Jewish framework. Both Lk and Mt show the descent from David. The fact that neither genealogy can bear close historical examination must not be held against the evangelists; they were only following the custom of the period. Genealogies of the same type are to be found in the Old Testament.

3:23. *About thirty years old.* Figures of this kind, like genealogies were not meant to be taken literally. It is a statement to imply that Jesus was mature and ready to begin his public ministry.

4. Temptation in the wilderness (Mk 1:12–13; Mt 4:1–11).

The divine Son of God accepted the limitations of our humanity (Philippians 2:7) and experienced temptation as we do (Hebrews 2:17–18; 4:14–16). He withdrew to the wilderness to think out what his task as Messiah involved.

4:1. *Filled with the Holy Spirit, Jesus left* . . . The part played by the Holy Spirit is again given prominence.

3. *If you are the Son of God.* The devil tried to sow doubt in the mind of Jesus. See also v. 9.
Tell this stone to turn into a loaf. (i) Jesus had divine power which ordinary people do not possess. He could use it to save himself from the pain and weariness natural to humanity. On the cross he was told to save himself if he was the Christ; he refused to use his power for himself. (ii) The people who thronged Jesus would be the poor, the hungry, and the sick; he could spend most of his time dealing with their physical needs.

4. *Man does not live on bread alone* (Deuteronomy 8:3). The passage continues, 'but . . . on everything that proceeds from the mouth of Yahweh'. i.e. The vital need of the people was spiritual, not physical.

5. *The devil showed him* . . . *the kingdoms of the world.* Earthly kingdoms were won and depended for their continuance on armed force, wealth, and the cleverness of the king in using events and people to his own advantage. All were under the authority of the devil.

4:7. *Worship me.* To worship really means to give first place in your regard to; the devil was suggesting that Jesus should use the customary methods for winning power and keeping it. If Jesus had wished, he could have headed a rebellion and driven out the Romans; he could, in short, have been the political kind of Messiah expected by the Jews.

8. *You must worship the Lord your God* (Deuteronomy 6:13). The ways of God are the opposite of the devil's ways. Jesus had come to serve God by serving mankind, and demonstrating totally fresh values.

9. *He led him to Jerusalem . . .* A test of this kind would have enabled Jesus to live in certain knowledge of his identity; he would not have had to work things out in faith as men must. (The agony in the garden 22:39–46.)

12. *You must not put the Lord your God to the test* (Deuteronomy 6:16).

III. THE GALILEAN MINISTRY

Jesus begins to preach

14. *Jesus with the power of the Spirit . . .* Lk places great emphasis on this (3:22, 4:1).
Jesus at Nazareth (Mk 6:1–6; Mt 13:53–58)

The rapid change in the attitude of the people to Jesus in this story, is puzzling at first. Lk may have combined the account of three separate visits to Nazareth in such a way as to symbolise the ministerial experience of Jesus as a whole. (i) First he was honoured vv. 16–22. (ii) Then people became bewildered because they thought they knew all about Jesus and found that they did not, vv. 23–24. (iii) Finally Jesus met with active hostility and rejection as the force of his message penetrated, vv. 25–30.

The description of synagogue procedure is unique in the New Testament. Lk brings out again the fact that Jesus conformed to religious custom; he went into the synagogue on the sabbath as he usually did (2:21–24; 41f.).

4:16. *Nazara.* A rare form of the name 'Nazareth'.

17. *They handed him the scroll.* Any man of note in the congregation might be invited to read the Scriptures and speak afterwards.

18. *The spirit of the Lord has been given to me* (Isaiah 61:1–2). The text is aptly preceded by the statement in v. 14.

22. *Joseph's son.* Lk is suggesting the contrast between what was supposed (3:23) and what was the truth about the parentage of Jesus. See Mk 6:3 for another version of what was said.

26. *A widow at Zarephath.* Like Naaman the Syrian, v. 27, she was a heathen. The stories (I Kings 17:8–24; II Kings 5:1–19), illustrate the care of Yahweh (God) for the heathen nations, a matter of much interest to Lk.

28. *Everyone was enraged.* Like the Old Testament prophets, Jesus had insisted that Israel had been chosen not for privilege but for responsibility, and the idea that Yahweh preferred the heathen to disobedient Israel was intolerable.

30. *He slipped through the crowd.* The initiative was always with Jesus and it was not yet time for his arrest and death. This is a point that is stressed in the Fourth Gospel.

4:31–6:16. This section is based on Mk 1:21–3:6 except for the story of the miraculous catch 5:1–7 found only in Lk.

MIRACLES

Belief in the miraculous powers of Jesus is an essential part of the gospel message. Attempts to minimise or explain them away are not uncommon, but if Jesus was no more than a great teacher who was tragically put to death, his impact on his own and subsequent generations is incomprehensible.

(i) The miracles are signs of the power and loving kindness of God.

(ii) They are visual aids to comprehension of God's activity in the mental and spiritual spheres. The cleansings show God's power to cleanse from sin; the restoration of sight points to the renewal of capacity to see the truth; and since hearing and obeying are equivalents in the Old Testament, the healing of the deaf represents return to obedience to God.

Jesus teaches in Capernaum and cures a demoniac

4:31. *Capernaum.* The town was on the shore of the Lake of Galilee, an important customs post on the route to coast from the east. It was the home of Simon and Andrew and the two sons of Zebedee, James and John.

32. *He spoke with authority.* It was both the quality of his teaching and his authority which struck people. Unlike the scribes (Intro B) what he had to say was fresh minted.

33. *Possessed by the spirit of an unclean devil.* The phrase should be understood precisely as it stands; devil possession, not mental illness was the trouble. Now, in our own day, there are priests specially trained to use exorcism (expel evil spirits), and they do it in Lon-

don, Paris, and New York, and not only among
primitive peoples.

4:34. *Have you come to destroy us?* This cure was perhaps
placed first in order to demonstrate the whole purpose
of Christ's coming, the freeing of mankind from the
power of evil.

Cure of Simon's mother-in-law

38. *Simon.* Simon Peter. See Mt 16:13–20 for the story of
how he got the second name, omitted by Lk.

A number of cures

40. *At sunset.* The sabbath ended at sunset, and only then
did the Law allow people to go any distance from
home, or to carry the sick.
Laying his hands on each he cured them. The laying on
of hands for the healing of the sick is still used by the
Church, and the patient is helped to cope with his illness if he is not actually cured. The word 'each' is
important; concern for the individual is one of the
hallmarks of Christianity.

41. *He . . . would not allow them to speak.* Perhaps Jesus
did not want great crowds coming to see what he
would do as if he were a magician: he wanted individuals to recognise that God was working through him.

Jesus leaves Capernaum and travels through Judaea

44. *Judaea.* This is in the south round Jerusalem; Lk was
using the word in the wide sense meaning the land of
Israel.

The first four disciples are called (Mk 1:16–20)

5:1. *The Lake of Gennesaret.* Galilee.

3. *Taught from the boat.* The arrangement kept the crowd
at a distance and the water also would act as a sound-
ing board.

5:4. *Pay out your nets for a catch.* See Jn 21. There may be a common source behind the two stories, Lk using what was in fact the story of a post-resurrection appearance as the story of the call of Simon Peter. 'Master' in v. 5 has become 'Lord' in v. 8.

8. *I am a sinful man.* Old Testament prophets reacted in just the same way when they were aware of the presence of God (Isaiah 6:1–8).

11. *It is men you will catch.* Again like the prophets in the Old Testament, the call was followed by a sending forth.

Cure of a leper

13. *Jesus touched him.* This is the first example of our Lord's attitude to the outcasts of society. The man's disease was disgusting and contagious and Jesus bridged the gap which separated him from normal life; he stretched out his hand and touched him.

14. *Tell no one.* See 4:41.

Show yourself to the priest. Again Jesus is seen as conforming to the requirements of the Law, giving instructions that it must be kept. For the regulations on cleansing see Leviticus 14.

16. *Where he could be alone and pray.* See 3:21; Mk 1:35.

THE CONFLICT STORIES 5:17–6:11
(Mk 2–3:6)

These stories illustrate the particular subjects of conflict between Jesus and the Jewish leaders. Each contains a pithy saying which underlines the point at issue, the question of the authority of Jesus being basic to all. The Pharisees were constantly on the watch because they regarded themselves as responsible for what the people were taught.

Cure of the paralytic

5:17. *Doctors of the Law*. Scribes (Intro B).
The power of the Lord, i.e. God.

19. *The tiles*. Lk did not belong to Palestine and imagined a house with a tiled roof such as he was accustomed to. Mk who belonged to the country, said they stripped the roof. Flat, and constructed of poles overlaid with reeds, that would be easy.

20. *Seeing their faith*. It was the faith of the friends, not of the sick man, which was effective, as in intercessory prayer.

20. *Your sins are forgiven you*. Jesus took the onlookers completely by surprise, not because he gave spiritual medicine to a man physically sick, but because he assumed the authority of God.

21. *Who is this man talking blasphemy?* Blasphemy was the worst sin, man making himself equal with God, and it was punishable by death. Who was the man? The story provides the answer.
Who can forgive sins but God alone? The nature of the 'Good News' begins to be clear. At 4:35, the healing of the demoniac, the evil will was expelled. The next stage in restoration is forgiveness, the blotting out of the past. The subject is particularly prominent in Lk 15:12–32; 23:34, 39–43.

24. *To prove to you*. (i) The physical healing showed the reality of the invisible healing effected by forgiveness. (ii) The authority of Jesus in both the physical and spiritual realms was clear.
The Son of Man. This title is one which Jesus used of himself and which only he himself used. 'Son of God' and 'Son of David' were both common titles for the

131

expected Messiah, and because he did not intend to play the expected part but one totally different, he adopted a title upon which fresh teaching could be grafted. The disciples were slow to understand as he told some of them after the resurrection (24:25–27). There are two main ideas to remember in connection with the title:

(i) It is associated with the description of the Suffering Servant in Isaiah, see 3:22, and therefore with ideas of the creative value of suffering, accepted and offered to God.

(ii) It is associated with the vision of Daniel (Daniel 7:13–14) and therefore with universal authority.

'I saw coming on the clouds of heaven
one like a son of man

* * * * * * *

On him was conferred sovereignty
glory and kingship
and men of all peoples, nations and languages
became his servants.'

5:26. *Filled with awe.* A mixture of reverence and wonder.

The call of Levi

27. *Levi.* From a very early date Levi was said to be Matthew, author of the first gospel (Mt 10:3). As a tax collector he had frequent dealings with the heathen and was therefore classed as a 'sinner' (Intro B2). He may well have been guilty of extortion because the position was bought and a large outlay had to be got back (19:1–10).

30. *Why do you eat and drink with tax collectors and sinners?* The second reason why Jesus was attacked by the authorities was because he ignored all the taboos and regulations that separated him, as a Jew, from other people. The real implication of the example of Jesus is in process of being grasped by the majority

of civilised people now for the first time in history as prejudices of class and race are increasingly recognised for what they are.

5:32. *I have not come to call the righteous but sinners to repentance.* Jesus was ironical. The self-satisfaction of the Pharisees prevented them from seeing their faults (3:8; 18:9–14).

Discussion on fasting

Fasting was part of Jewish religious discipline, as it is of most world religions; it is a means of learning to control physical appetite, and a sign of penitence. The fast on the Day of Atonement was the most important for the Jews, but fasting on other occasions had become customary and was regarded as praiseworthy. Our Lord's departure from convention in this matter was a third reason why the Pharisees quarrelled with him.

34. *The bridegroom.* Jesus was speaking of himself, and his death.

36. *This parable.* A commonplace in the natural world or in human activity is used as an example to convey a truth, generally about the kingdom of God.
The parable of the patch. New material cannot satisfactorily be used for patching because the new material pulls away from the old, and the tear gets worse: Mk 2:21 makes better sense of the saying than Lk. The meaning is that the life and teaching which Jesus brings, is totally new and cannot be fitted on to Judaism, the old religion.

37. *Nobody puts new wine into old skins.* New wine had to be put into new leather bottles which expanded with the fermentation. Old leather bottles, already fully stretched, would burst if new wine was put into them. The two parables have the same meaning.

133

Picking corn on the sabbath

6:1. *One sabbath.* All work was forbidden by the fourth
commandment (Exodus 20:8–11). The scribes had
elaborated the regulations.
Picking ears of corn. The disciples had been busy in
the service of God and having had no time for a meal,
satisfied their hunger as best they could. The owner of
the corn would not have objected.

3. *So you have not read . . .* Jesus referred the Pharisees to
the Scriptures which they thought they knew so well.
David was fleeing from Saul, and it was part of the
tradition that this particular episode happened on the
sabbath.

5. *The Son of Man is master of the sabbath.* This was a
tremendous assertion of authority. Jesus was above
the Law.

Cure of the man with the withered hand

If there was danger of death, the Law allowed medical
treatment to be given on the sabbath; this man was
not in danger. Jesus showed that compassion was to
be a guiding principle.

11. *They were furious.* See Mk 3:6. They discussed how to
destroy him.

The choice of the Twelve (Mk 3:13–19; Mt 10:1–4)

12. *He spent the whole night in prayer* (see 3:21; 5:16).
Jesus was about to establish a community of followers
which would later be known as the Church, his instru-
ment for the conversion of the world.

13. *He summoned his disciples.* The word 'disciple' means
'learner'; it also conveys the idea of 'follower'. They
learnt from Jesus by simply being with him as well as
by what he actually told them (Mk 3:14).

He . . . picked out twelve of them. There were twelve tribes in ancient Israel chosen by God to be 'a consecrated nation' (Exodus 19:6). The Church would be the new Israel and it would be the task of the Twelve to proclaim the gospel.

He called them apostles. 'Apostollos' is a Greek word used in the first century for a man sent out by a ruler as his representative, with full powers to act on his behalf, an ambassador. After the ascension the apostles acted on behalf of Christ, and they were prepared for this during his ministry (9:1f.; 10:1f.).

6:14. *Simon whom he called Peter* (Mt 16:13–20).
James and John. The sons of Zebedee (Lk 5:10; Mk 1:19–20).

15. *Matthew.* Generally identified with Levi (5:27).

The crowds follow Jesus

17. *Tyre and Sidon.* These were heathen cities of Phoenicia, on the coast. The crowd came from far and wide.

19. *Power came out of him that cured them all.* It is helpful to notice the sequence of events. The plot to kill Jesus (v. 11) was followed by the call of the Twelve and a demonstration of his mighty power. The process now begun can never be halted.

The inaugural discourse (Mt chs 5–7. The Sermon on the Mount)

This discourse is sometimes called the Sermon on the Plain to distinguish it from Mt's version which is longer and more Jewish. Lk left out material which would not have meant much to his Gentile readers. Lk and Mt are thought to have depended on the same source, Q. (Intro E). More important is that Jesus, having called the New Israel into being, v. 13, now provided the Law it was to live by, completing the

135

work of Moses who gave the elementary regulations at Sinai (Exodus 20).

The Beatitudes, i.e. 'What makes for blessedness'. In times of danger and persecution, the Jews had been comforted by the conviction that God, being good and faithful to His people, would deliver them in the end and reward them in His kingdom. Behind the Beatitudes there is the idea of present hardship and future bliss and they form a logical sequence.

6:20. *You who are poor.* In a time of crisis about three hundred years earlier, it was the poor who remained faithful to their Law while the rich had become tainted with the heathenism of foreign rulers. Thus 'poor' came to mean 'saintly' and 'the rich' were the worldly and irreligious. The poor therefore are happy having accepted God's will as their rule of life, and as citizens of His kingdom they have the privileges of citizenship.

21. *Happy you who are hungry now.* The contrast between the present and the good time coming with the establishment of the kingdom of God, is as different as a famine from a feast. 'Man does not live on bread alone, but on everything that proceeds from the mouth of Yahweh' (4:3). Those who are aware of the contrast between their own lives and the conditions around them, with what should be, will eventually find satisfaction.

22. *Happy you who weep now.* This is a second contrast conveying the same idea. Present and future are as different as tears from laughter. The saints are homesick for the kingdom. 'Our citizenship is in heaven' (Philippians 3:20).

23. *Happy are you when people hate you.* The saints' beliefs and way of life would be objectionable to the worldly and irreligious who would resort to persecution. This had been the experience of the prophets in the past; it would be the experience of the followers of Jesus.

The curses

These are addressed to the worldly and irreligious who reject the kingdom. Materialists caring only for wealth and physical pleasure, they will find that these things offer no defence in adversity: in age, sickness, and at death.

Love of enemies

Love is the first requirement of Christ's Law (I Corinthians 13). It is quite distinct from sentiment and liking which depend upon the kind of people we happen to be. It springs from the direction of the will, and is expressed in kindness and compassion to everyone without exception.

6:29. *Present the other cheek*. There is to be no counter-attack or attempt at revenge. Jesus is dealing here with personal relationships. He is not saying that evil, cruelty, and injustice must be suffered without protest. *Do not refuse your tunic*. The gift would leave the owner naked. This extreme example provides the measure of what Christian giving should be.

31. *Treat others as you would like them to treat you*. This is sometimes called the Golden Rule. It is found also in the teachings of the Buddha in the sixth century B.C.

34. *What thanks can you expect?* Do you expect God to be particularly pleased with you? Kindness at the fifty-fifty level is less than the width and generosity of love.

35. *Sons of the Most High*. The disciples will be sons because they reflect God's way with mankind: they have the family likeness.

137

Compassion and generosity

6:36. *Be compassionate.* Compassion means 'suffering with', involvement and participation in the adversity of others. It entails action as well as the emotion of pity. The parable of the Good Samaritan is the classic illustration of what compassion is (10:29–37).

37. *Do not judge.* This follows on logically from the command to be compassionate. Only God has the knowledge to pass judgement. We can hate the sin without judging the sinner.

38. *Give.* The wrong-doer is not only to be forgiven. He is to be shown active kindness as well.
A full measure . . . will be poured into your lap. The loose garment pouched over the belt, served as a bag for grain bought in the market. A merchant would give generous weight to any other who was generous to him. God's overflowing kindness far surpasses what man would give to man.

Integrity

39. *Can one blind man guide another?* Sinners are not qualified to judge others (v. 37) and neither are they qualified to tell others what their duty is.

40. *The disciple is not superior to his teacher.* The disciple will only be a safe guide when he has humbly accepted instruction from Christ, and tried to put it into practice.

41–2. *The splinter and the plank.* The point is further underlined. Self-criticism and reform are essential prerequisites for anyone attempting to guide others.

43–5. *A man's words flow out of what fills his heart.* The meaning seems to be that a man's influence depends on what he is and what he does, much more than any advice he may feel moved to give. You judge the tree by the kind of fruit it produces. The command not to

judge (v. 37) is amplified by this passage; persons may
not be judged, but it is commonsense to estimate as
good or bad, both actions and words.

The true disciple

6:46. *Why do you call me 'Lord, Lord' and not do what I say?*
This is lip service, the opposite of integrity.

48–9. *The two foundations.* On the one hand the foundations
are laid on rock after deep digging. On the other, they
are non-existent, the walls being built from the surface
of the ground only.
The river. This represents acute personal crisis of
some kind, temptation perhaps or adversity. The man
who listened to the teaching and always tried to act on
it, survived the crisis because of his integrity, his
wholeheartedness. The other man went under because
he was divided within himself.

Cure of the centurion's servant (Mt 8:5–13; Jn 4:43–
54)

7:1. *Capernaum.* See 4:31.

2. *A centurion.* He belonged to the Roman army of occu-
pation and must have been a God-fearer (Intro C)
since he had built a synagogue for the community. For
another of the same type see Acts 10, and the one
present at the crucifixion (23:47).

3. *Jewish elders.* They held responsibilities in the local
congregation.

6. *Do not put youself to trouble.* He was considerate; he
knew that entry into his house would mean defilement
for a Jew. Anyway, his faith was such that he did not
think it necessary for Jesus to come.

8. *For I am under authority myself.* He was used to obey
and to be obeyed, and he recognised authority when
he encountered it.

7:10. *Not even in Israel.* The Jews are compared adversely with the Gentiles, a theme which runs through the gospel (4:25–27).
The messengers . . . found the servant in perfect health. The miracle is an example of the power of Jesus to heal from a distance.

The son of the widow of Nain restored to life (Lk only)

12. *The only son.* She was a very pitiable figure because she was a widow and there was no one now to support her.

13. *The Lord.* Lk uses the title hitherto strictly reserved for Yahweh, God.

16. *Everyone was filled with awe.* It was the same after the healing of the paralytic (5:26). The story of the raising of Jairus's daughter (8:40–56) is common to all the synoptic gospels. The raising of Lazarus, the only other miracle of this type, is in St John (Jn 11).

The Baptist's question (Mt 11:2–19)

The Baptist was in prison (3:19–20) and perhaps for that reason needed reassurance.

22. *Go back and tell John what you have seen and heard.* John would recognise the allusion of Jesus to prophetic passages in Isaiah (26:19; 35:5–6; 61:1) and would know that he was indeed the Messiah. See 4:18 for the text of the sermon of Jesus at Nazareth.

26. *Much more than a prophet.* He was the messenger foretold by Malachi (3:1) who would prepare the way for the Messiah. See the words of Gabriel to Zechariah (1:17).

28. *The least in the kingdom of God is greater than he.* John belonged to the old order of things. The most humble of the disciples of Jesus had an immense advantage over him.

7:29. *The people . . . and the tax collectors too acknowledged God's plan.* But the Pharisees did not. Rejection of John led to rejection of Jesus.

Jesus condemns his contemporaries

32. *We played the pipes.* The children's song was about a game of weddings and funerals which got no response from the audience either way.

35. *Wisdom has been proved right by all her children.* The contemporaries of Jesus were like the children's audience; neither John the Baptist nor Jesus in their different ways could please them. But the true children of God recognised both John and Jesus.

The woman who was a sinner (Lk only)

Simon was a typically virtuous Pharisee; the woman was an outcast, contact with whom defiled a Jew who was careful to observe the Law.

41–2. *There was once a creditor.* This little parable teaches the moral of the whole story. The experience of forgiveness results in love, and the greater the awareness of the need for forgiveness, the greater the love.

44. *You poured no water over my feet.* Elementary courtesy required this, and anointing was the custom if the guest was specially distinguished. Simon had been very remiss.

48. *Your sins are forgiven.* See the cure of the paralytic (5:20).

50. *Your faith has saved you.* 'Faith' in the gospels means 'trust', trust in Jesus. However she had first come into contact with Jesus, she had responded with trust and so is the type of the true disciple (6:46) who having heard, obeyed.

141

The women accompanying Jesus

8:2. *Mary surnamed the Magdalene.* The surname probably indicates that she came from the town of Magdala. In the Middle Ages she was always identified
with the woman who was a sinner (7:36–50), but
modern scholars do not accept that.

Seven demons. Seven, like the other numbers mentioned (3:23, 4:2), is not to be taken literally; it represents completeness. Mary had been in an extreme
state of devil possession.

3. *Joanna the wife of Herod's steward.* In Acts 13:1 Lk
mentions Manean, Herod's foster brother, as being a
member of the church at Antioch, a city which Lk
knew well and which may even have been his home.
Manean therefore may have provided Lk with information. Joanna and Mary were both at the tomb after
the resurrection (24:10).

Suzanna and several others who provided for them.
Suzanna is not mentioned anywhere else in the Gospels. It was not unusual for rabbis (teachers) to be
supported by contributions from women, but they
spoke to them as little as possible as it was not considered desirable. Lk's mention of the women here,
and as having watched the crucifixion from afar
(24:10), suggests that Jesus took as little notice of
conventions in this connection, as in the case of
'sinners' and lepers.

8:4–9:50

In this section, Lk now makes use of a second block of
Marcan material; Mk 4:1–9:40, but omitting Mk
6:45–7:23 as perhaps not being of value to Gentile
readers.

Parable of the sower

At the end of the inaugural discourse (6:46–49) Jesus
spoke of the true disciple as one who having heard the

teaching, put it into practice. In this parable, he considers the different types of hearers under the figure of different types of ground, and suggests what are the obstacles which prevent development in discipleship. The emphasis comes at the end; a splendid crop was harvested eventually in spite of what happened to some of the seed. The parable gives a summary of missionary experience which has always been true.

Why Jesus speaks in parables

These verses are difficult, and generally acknowledged to be so.

8:10. *The mysteries of the kingdom of God.* Jesus never provided his hearers with plain statements either about the kingdom, or himself; he gave them suggestions which he left them to work out for themselves. The disciples having responded to his call, and being constantly in his company were growing aware of what the kingdom of God was, what was required of its members, and of the work of the Messiah in it.
For the rest there are only parables. The rest, not having accepted Jesus, could make nothing of his teaching. The quotation from Isaiah 6:9 was always interpreted by the first Christians as referring to the Jews who rejected Christ.

The parable of the sower explained

12. *Then the devil comes.* Our Lord accepted the common belief in an active and personal spirit of evil abroad in the world, working through the weakness of human beings to obstruct the will of God (4:1–13, 33–36).
In case they should believe and be saved. i.e. In case they should be converted. After Pentecost 'to believe and be saved' was the phrase in common use. Belief in Jesus as Lord had to be declared before baptism, as in the Church today (Acts 16:31).

143

8:13. *In time of trial they give up.* The trial is not difficulty or adversity, but the test of persecution. Under persecution they deny the faith they have affirmed; they become apostates.

15. *Perseverance.* Hearing is combined with doing.

Parable of the lamp

16. *A lamp . . . on a lampstand.* The lamp gives light to people entering the house. The Gospel is like a shining light attracting people from outside (the gentiles) into the Church.

17. *Nothing is hidden.* All the mysteries of the kingdom of God (v. 10) will be made clear.

18. *Take care how you hear.* The disciple must listen humbly because he is not superior to his teacher (6:40). He must put into practice what is learnt and so grow in understanding.
    From anyone who has not. This is a difficult saying, but the meaning may be that as gifts of mind and manual skills deteriorate if they are not used, so the capacity to understand the Gospel weakens by neglect.

19–21. *The true kinsmen of Jesus*
    Lk has taken this passage out of its context in Mk 3:31–35 to serve as a conclusion to this section on parables. He has slightly changed the saying in v. 21 to emphasize the double aspect of obedience, hearing and doing. It is by obedience that men come into a close relationship with Jesus: this relationship is the essence of what is meant by Christianity.
    The calming of the storm (Mk 4:35–41)
    Mk's account brings out the force of this story which Lk has softened in the telling.

24. *Master, master.* The disrespectful question in Mk, 'Do you not care?' has been left out, possibly because Lk

had to summarise but no doubt also because he did not want to present the disciples in a bad light.

He . . . rebuked the wind and rough water. In Mk, Jesus said, 'Quiet now,' which are the words he addressed to the demoniac (4:31–37; Mk 1:21–28). The story therefore illustrates the authority of Jesus over the demonic forces in nature, as in man. This is the authority ascribed to God by the prophets of the Old Testament.

8:25. *Where is your faith?* Trust in Jesus (7:50). The command to obedience brought out in the preceding section is now linked with the demand for faith. Obedience to the rulers of the kingdoms of the world stemmed from fear; in the kingdom of God it was to grow from trust.

They were awestruck. A point constantly made in the gospels.

The Gerasene demoniac

The general indications are that Jesus was in gentile country; the place was on the eastern and heathen side of Lake Galilee, the man addressed Jesus in terms that a pagan might have used—son of the Most High God; and pigs were kept, a thing which Jews would not do.

29. *Jesus had been telling . . .* Jesus began to work on the man as soon as he saw him, as he stepped ashore (v. 27).

30. *What is your name?* Jesus asked this either as part of the process of exorcism (expulsion of the evil spirit), or to remind the man of his true self.

31. *The Abyss.* The depths of the earth, the usual dwelling place of demons.

35. *They found the man . . . sitting at the feet of Jesus.* The attitude was that of the convert and disciple.

8:39. *Go back home . . . and report all.* Because this was gentile country there was no danger that the people would try to rally round Jesus as a political leader, as the kind of Messiah that he did not choose to be.
Report all that God has done for you. It is interesting to compare this passage with Acts 2:22, Peter's sermon at Pentecost.

Cure of the woman with a haemorrhage; Jairus' daughter raised (Mk 5:21–43)

40. *On his return.* Jesus was back in Jewish territory.

43. *A woman . . . whom no one had been able to cure.* Lk has left out Mk's implied criticism of the doctors.

45. *Master, it is the crowds round you pushing.* As in the story of the calming of the storm, the blunt character of the disciples' words have been modified. Lk mentions Peter particularly.

46. *I felt that power had gone out from me.* Mk does not explain how Jesus knew what had happened.

47. *The woman came forward trembling.* Her disease made her ceremonially unclean, and she was legally at fault in touching so much as the fringe of his cloak.

48. *Your faith has restored you to health.* This woman was restored to health of body by faith; the woman in the house of Simon the Pharisee was restored to health of soul by faith (6:36–50).

50. *Do not be afraid, only have faith.* A supreme example of the power of faith is to be given.

51. *Peter and John and James* (5:1–11). These three disciples figure most prominently in the gospels, and it is characteristic of Lk to place John before James.

56. *He ordered them not to tell anyone.* There is the usual command to secrecy.

9. The mission of the Twelve

The raising of the son of the widow of Nain (7:11–17) was followed by the reply of Jesus to the inquiry of John the Baptist, and the clear indication as to his identity. The second raising from the dead (8:49–56) was followed by the extension of Christ's work through the agency of the apostles.

9:1. *He . . . gave them power and authority* (6:13). The apostles were empowered to do exactly the same things that Jesus had been doing; casting out devils, healing the sick, and proclaiming the kingdom. In sending them out, Jesus was training them for the time after his ascension and the outpouring of the Holy Spirit (Acts 2:1–13), when they would spread the Gospel without his physical presence to help them.

3. *Take nothing for your journey.* They were to trust in God and their converts for their basic needs.

4. *Whatever house you enter, stay there.* They were to be simple and direct. There was to be no picking and choosing.

5. *Shake the dust from your feet as a sign.* It was an age-old gesture indicating broken relationship (Acts 13:51).
Herod and Jesus (Mk 6:14–16). See also Intro B and 3:18. The work of Jesus was a continuation of the work of John the Baptist, the baptism of Jesus showing the link.

The return of the apostles; Miracle of the loaves (Mk 6:30–44)

10. *Bethsaida.* Mk says they went to a lonely place, and in spite of his mention of a town, Lk clearly describes the miracle in the same setting.

13. *We have no more than five loaves* . . . As in the story of the storm on the lake (8:22–25), and in that of the

147

woman's cure (8:40–48), Lk has again modified Mk's account, making the speech of the disciples much more respectful.

9:16. *Then he took the five loaves* . . . The fact that this miracle is also recorded by Jn who makes no mention of other miracles common to the synoptic gospels, indicates its importance. It was always associated in the minds of the early Christians with the institution of the Eucharist (Holy Communion), as the discourse on the bread of life in the synagogue at Capernaum shows (Jn 6:22–63). The Jews believed that the kingdom of the Messiah would be ushered in with a great banquet known as the Messianic banquet, and the feeding of the five thousand seemed to be it: the idea lies behind the second beatitude (6:21).
He took . . . (*he blessed*) . . . *he broke* . . . (*he gave*). These are significant actions performed by Jesus at the institution of the Eucharist (22:19–20).

17. *They all ate as much as they wanted.* Only God can satisfy man's deepest hunger (Psalm 16:11; 107:9).
Twelve baskets. The provision of Jesus was superabundant. There was enough for all of the new Israel who would have their origin in Christ (6:13).
Fish. The fish became the symbol of Christianity, used as a secret sign in times of persecution. Not only was it a reminder of the miracle, but also the five letters in the Greek word for fish, were the first letters of the five Greek words meaning Jesus Christ, Son of God, Saviour.

Peter's profession of faith (Mk 8:27–38)

Mk says that Jesus and the disciples were near Caesarea Philippi, in the far north, a detail omitted by Lk but useful to bear in mind because of the division of the gospel at 9:50 and the beginning of Section IV. The Journey to Jerusalem.

9:18. *He was praying alone* (3:21; 5:16; 6:12).
Who do the crowds say that I am? By means of his question Jesus brought the disciples to face the mystery of his identity, and form their own conclusion.

19. *John the Baptist . . . Elijah . . . one of the ancient prophets.* To say these names was enough to know that they were totally inadequate to explain Jesus.

20. *It was Peter who spoke up.* Peter was the leader of the apostles (Mt 16:13–20). After the crucifixion he was to strengthen his brethren (22:32).
'*The Christ of God.*' This was a tremendous discovery. Jesus was the long-awaited deliverer.

21. *He gave them strict orders not to tell.* The crowds, all agog for a political deliverer, could not be trusted with the information. They were not ready to be told how he was going to fulfil his mission, and even the Twelve would fail to understand, though it was from this point in the ministry that he began to teach them that his redeeming work entailed suffering, rejection, and death.

First prophecy of the Passion

The word 'Passion' is derived from the Latin and means 'Suffering'; it is used exclusively in this connection because Christ's suffering was unique.

22. *The Son of Man.* For the significance of this title see note on 3:22; 5:24. The idea of the creative power and value of suffering accepted and offered to God is of great importance in Christian thinking.

In his account of this episode, Lk has omitted Peter's protest and the stern rebuke of Jesus (Mk 8:31–33; Mt 16:21–23).

The condition of following Christ

23. *If anyone wants to be a follower of mine, let him renounce himself.* Discipleship is costly. Worldly objectives, wealth and power, must be given up (4:5–8).

And take up his cross. Crucifixion was the Roman
method of execution, and crosses lined the roadsides.
Originally this saying was probably a warning of the
likely cost of discipleship (Mk 8:24), but by the time
Lk wrote it was understood metaphorically as the
words 'every day' show. The cross of the Christian is
made up of all the factors demanding self-discipline in
obedience to Christ.

9:24. *Anyone who wants to save his life will lose it* (6:20–26).
'The rich,' self-centred and caring only for power and
wealth, will lose the joys of citizenship in the kingdom
of God.
Anyone who loses his life for my sake . . . He may
actually die for Christ, or lay aside worldly position
for Christ, but in either case he gains life with Christ.

26. *If anyone is ashamed of me and my words . . .* The
thought here is of the man who denies faith in Christ
because of persecution.
When he comes in his own glory. From this and similar
sayings, the first Christians believed that the end of
the world was near, and that Jesus would return in
great glory to establish the kingdom of God. The
return was called the Parousia, and there is evidence
for the belief in some of St Paul's letters.

The kingdom will come

27. *Some . . . will not taste death before they see the kingdom.* This was understood to mean that the Parousia
would happen in the lifetime of the apostles. As it
was delayed, however, the belief gained ground that
the kingdom comes into being in the present, as
people accept Christ and try to obey him, an idea
brought out in St John's Gospel.

The Transfiguration

28. *About eight days after this.* The mention of a definite length of time indicates the importance of the connection between Peter's profession of faith, the prophecy of the Passion, and the transfiguration; Mk says there was an interval of six days between the two events.

9:29. *As he prayed . . .* (3:21; 5:16; 6:12; 9:18).
The aspect of his face was changed. The disciples saw him in the glory which he left to be born as man, and to which he would return after his death and resurrection (Philippians 2:6–11).

30. *Moses and Elijah.* These men represent the Law and the Prophets respectively, all that was best in the old religion which came to perfection in Christ.

31. *They were speaking of his passing.* The word used in the Greek is 'exodos'. As Moses had led Israel out of Egypt (the exodus) into the Promised Land, so Christ by his departure would lead the New Israel into the kingdom of God.

33. *Let us make three tents.* The Feast of Tabernacles in the autumn celebrated the grape harvest, and it was customary to camp in the vineyards in temporary shelters. Peter wanted to make such shelters in order to prolong a wonderful experience.

34. *A cloud came.* In the Old Testament, the cloud is the symbol of the presence and glory of God, provided in His mercy because no one could see Him and live (Exodus 40:34).

35. *This is my Son, the Chosen One.* These were the words spoken at the baptism of Jesus (3:22). He is the Anointed of God and his mysterious statement about his suffering, rejection, and death is confirmed as true. 'Listen to him.'

This section 9:10–36, foreshadows the major events in the Passion Narrative. The miracle of the loaves prefigures the Lord's Supper; the prophecy of the Passion points to the rejection and crucifixion of Jesus; the transfiguration looks forward to his ascension and glory, and confirms that he is the Son of God to whom obedience is due. It is a good illustration of the way an ancient writer interpreted his material while at the same time recording events.

The epileptic demoniac

9:40. *I begged your disciples . . . and they could not.* Only three disciples had been with Jesus on the mountain; this story emphasises the failure in faith of all those people who hung on the words of Jesus and admired him, but failed to translate the hearing into doing. They were 'faithless and perverse'.

43. *Everyone was awestruck by the greatness of God.* Lk brings out strongly the authority and power of Christ in contrast to the disciples. At the same time he underlines the mystery in the prophecy of his suffering since Christ's superiority in the most adverse situation was so clearly demonstrated.

Second prophecy of the Passion

The prophecy was made the more emphatic by repetition as well as the extent of the disciples' failure in understanding. They were like 'the rest' (8:10), who were incapable of understanding the mysteries of the kingdom.

Who is the greatest?

46. *An argument started . . .* This illustrated the fact that the disciples were still thinking in terms of a political Messiah, and authority for themselves, and the degree to which they had failed to grasp the teaching of Jesus.

47. *He took a little child.* The child was an object lesson in humility, and the last words of v. 48 bring out the

point. 'The least among you all, that is the one who is
great.'

9:48. *Anyone who welcomes this little child in my name* . . .
This is one of the fundamental lessons of Christ. Ser-
vice to one's neighbour is service to Christ (10:29–37;
Mt 25:31–46).

IV. THE JOURNEY TO JERUSALEM

In this section, 9:51–19:27, Lk has kept to the
framework of Mk, but expanded it to include
material from 'Q', the sayings source also used
by Mt, and much important matter found nowhere
else. The disciples having recognised the fact that
he was the long-awaited Messiah, Jesus used the
journey southwards to Jerusalem as an opportunity to get them used to the idea that he was going
to suffer, be rejected, and killed, and to teach
them about the characteristics required in citizens
of the kingdom.

A Samaritan village is inhospitable (Lk only)

51. *The road for Jerusalem.* It was near the time of Passover when it was the duty of all Jews to be in Jerusalem. Jesus 'resolutely took the road' because he knew
that he was going to his death.

52. *A Samaritan village.* Jesus was disregarding normal
Jewish custom in planning to stay in a Samaritan
village. Jews despised Samaritans because (a) they
were of foreign extraction, the region having been
settled with foreign prisoners after the Assyrian con-
quest in the 8th century B.C. (II Kings 17) and (b)
though the Samaritans were Jews by religion, they
had broken away from the Jews of Judaea and built a
temple for themselves on Mt Gerizim. Jerusalem Jews

considered this blasphemous because Scripture said that there was to be only one temple, and that at Jerusalem.

9:53. *The people would not receive him.* The dislike was mutual

54. *James and John.* Surnamed Boanerges, sons of thunder (Mk 3:17). This incident suggests the reason. They expected Jesus to act like Elijah (II Kings 1:10–12).

Hardships of the apostolic calling

58. (1) *Foxes have holes.* The disciple must be ready to do without a place he can call 'home'.

60. (2) *Leave the dead . . . go and spread the news.* The most important family obligation is secondary to obligations to God.

62. (3) *No man . . . looking back . . . is fit.* The affairs of the kingdom are urgent. There must be no divided loyalty or hanging back.

The mission of the seventy-two disciples (Lk only)

10. The mission was to Samaria and seems to foreshadow the mission of the universal Church. Of the four gospels, only Lk and Jn mention Jesus as having been in Samaria. In some translations the number of disciples is given as seventy.

1. *In pairs, to all the towns and places he himself was to visit.* They were to go ahead, not to prepare lodgings as in 9:52, but to prepare people for the coming of Jesus. In Acts also, the apostles are represented as going out in pairs.

2. *The harvest is rich.* This saying is echoed in Jn 4:35, a passage also about Jesus in Samaria.

4. *Carry no purse . . . salute no one.* Their business was urgent, and all inessentials were to be dispensed with.

10:7. *Food and drink*. This command may refer to the strict Jewish food laws, non-observance of which made you a 'sinner' (Leviticus 11). The disciples were to accept without question whatever was put before them.

12. *Sodom*. This city is always representative of evil, and often linked with Gomorrah, its neighbour. Lot, nephew of Abraham lived nearby. Both cities were destroyed with brimstone and fire by Yahweh because of their iniquity.

13. *Chorazin: Bethsaida*. These cities were just north of Lake Galilee.
Tyre and Sidon. Pagan cities of Phoenicia on the coast (Mk 7:24–30).

16. *Anyone who listens to you, listens to me* (9:48)

True cause for the apostles to rejoice

17. *When we use your name*. In the Old Testament literature, names are more than mere labels; they indicate the nature of the bearer. Yahweh means 'I AM WHO I AM'; Jacob, the cunning one, changed his name and became Israel when he had wrestled with God. In the New Testament therefore, to speak or act in the name of Jesus means to identify with him to the fullest possible extent, and so with God. See Acts 3:16 and v. 16 above.

19. *The whole strength of the enemy* (Ephesians 6:10–20). Discipleship entails spiritual struggle against evil in all its forms.

20. *Your names are written in heaven*. The idea that Yahweh kept a record of acts done by His servants goes a long way back (Malachi 3:16).

The Good News revealed to the simple; The Father and the Son

This passage is reminiscent both in style and content of Jn. Mt also makes use of it (Mt 11:25–27).

10:21. *Learned and clever . . . mere children.* Because of their relationship with Jesus and trusting obedience, simple people have a spiritual insight denied to the learned.

The great commandment

25. *Eternal life.* This expression is often understood as meaning endless life, something which might be terrible. In fact it describes a quality of life, life with God (Psalm 16:11).

26. *What is written in the Law?* Again Jesus is seen as leading men to the truth by asking a question (9:18).

27. *You must love the Lord your God* (Deuteronomy 6:5). *Love your neighbour as yourself* (Leviticus 19:18). These two commandments were cited by Jesus himself as comprising the whole Law and the Prophets (Mt 22:34–40).

Parable of the good Samaritan (Lk only)

30. *From Jerusalem to Jericho.* It was a lonely road running through deep gorges down to the Jordan Valley.

31. *A priest.* He would have become ceremonially unclean if he touched a dead man, and preferred not to investigate. The same was true of the Levite, a Temple servant, v. 32.

33. *A Samaritan* (9:52). The point to notice is the total identification of the Samaritan with the distressed person, and his disregard of all barriers.

34. *Oil and wine.* The oil was soothing and the wine was antiseptic.
Martha and Mary (Lk only)
Of the Synoptists, only Lk mentions these two sisters. But Jn tells the story of the raising from the dead of their brother Lazarus (Jn 11:1–44), and says that they lived at Bethany just outside Jerusalem. Lk thinks of them as living much further north; he has a great deal

to recount before he tells of the arrival of Jesus in the neighbourhood of the Holy City.

10:40. *Martha was distracted with all the serving.* She meant very well, but fussed about little things. She provides a contrast with the Samaritan who was also active, but about what mattered, and in the right way.

42. *Mary has chosen the better part.* She had been sitting at the Lord's feet and listening to him. She represents contemplative discipleship, the counterpart of active discipleship. Mary's was the 'better part' because hearing must precede doing (6:40, 47).

The Lord's prayer

11 Mary's quietness and receptiveness composed the attitude of prayer; instruction is now given on what to say when we pray. Mt's version of the prayer (Mt 6:9–13) has seven clauses to Lk's five, and is the one which has always been used in the public worship of the Church.

1. *He was in a certain place praying* (3:21; 5:16; 6:12; 9:18, 29).

2. *Father.* This is the intimate form of address used in the family circle, 'Abba' in Aramaic (Mk 14:36). No ordinary Jew would have used the word in prayer, but the belief that God cares as a human father cares, was so strongly linked with the teaching and practice of Jesus, that the early Church used both words, Abba and Father (Romans 8:15, Galatians 4:6).
May your name be held holy (10:17). God is asked that His rule may be acknowledged everywhere, and all the moral values associated with Him.

3. *Our daily bread.* There is doubt about the meaning of the Greek word used here, but the petition is for the food necessary to enable us to work, food for the body and food for the soul. Jesus described himself as the

true bread (Jn 6:32). Some early versions have a different clause here: 'May your Holy Spirit come down on us and cleanse us.'

11:4. *In debt*. A Jewish expression for being in any kind of wrong.
Do not put us to the test. The thought here is of persecution when loyalty may be undermined. Nobody knows, until the test comes, how steadfast he can be.

The importunate friend (Lk only)

5. *Lend me three loaves*. It was a simple domestic emergency.

8. *Persistence will be enough*. This is the main point of the story. If a neighbour, much against his will, can be persuaded to help, we can be sure that the Father will listen to our requests.

Effective prayer (Mt 7:7–11)

9. *Ask . . . search . . . knock*. There is to be effort in prayer and alertness for the response.

11. *What father . . . would hand his son a stone . . . for bread?* A responsible earthly father does not give his child everything he asks, and neither does God. But in the process of asking for things in prayer, wants are often modified or no longer seem desirable, others being substituted. This process is as much an answer to prayer as the exact granting of a request.

13. *The Holy Spirit*. This is the supreme gift because he leads us into all truth (Jn 16:13; Intro E).

Jesus and Beelzebul (Mk 3:22–27; Mt 12:22–29)

14. *A devil and it was dumb*. It was believed that the patient's condition was the result of the demon's activity.

15. *Beelzebul*. Identified here with Satan, this was the

name of a Philistine god. Jesus was accused of black magic.

11:20. *The finger of God*, i.e. the power of God. The kingdom of God is already present with the coming of Christ.

21. *A strong man fully armed.* Satan seems strong and has many in his grip.

22. *Someone stronger.* Christ has come to conquer Satan and free his prisoners (4:31–34).

No compromise

23. The war against the power of Satan is real, and there can be no standing on the sidelines. The idea that life presents a clear-cut choice between good and evil, runs through the whole Bible (Deuteronomy 30:15–19; Lk 6:46–49; 12:51; Ephesians 6:10–17).

Return of the unclean spirit (Mt 12:43–45)

24. *Waterless country.* It was commonly believed at that time that the desert was the home of demons. When Jesus went into the wilderness to be tempted (4:1–13) he went into the stronghold of evil.

26. *Seven other spirits.* Eight would be able to resist another exorcism more easily than one alone. Exorcism alone was not enough; it was necessary that relationship with Jesus should be established as illustrated in the story of Legion (8:26–39).

The truly happy

27. *Happy the womb that bore you.* This was a common form of flattery which Jesus met with sharp practicality; he wanted his hearers to translate his teaching into action.

The sign of Jonah (Mt 12:38–42)

For the brief story of Jonah, see the Old Testament book under that name.

11:30. *Jonah became a sign to the Ninevites.* The people of Nineveh realised when they heard him preach, that he was sent by God, and repented: thus Jonah was himself a sign. Similarly Jesus the Son of Man was a sign to his contemporaries.

31. *The Queen of the South*, i.e. the Queen of Sheba (I Kings 10). Gentiles like the Ninevites and the Queen of Sheba are quick to respond to signs from God, and so will combine with them in condemning the contemporaries of Jesus.

The parable of the lamp repeated (8:16)

34. *The lamp of your body is your eye.* Physical eyesight is compared with spiritual understanding. There will be disaster if you suppose yourself to be clear-sighted when in reality you are blind.

36. *If . . . your whole body is filled with light.* A man illuminated by the Holy Spirit is like a lamp in the darkness to those around him (Mt 5:16). This light shines in Jesus (Jn 8:12)

The Pharisees and lawyers attacked

37. *A Pharisee invited him.* All the Pharisees were not hostile to Jesus (7:36f.).

38. *He had not first washed.* The ritual law required a ceremonial pouring of water over the hands before meals; it was not a matter of hygiene.

39. *You clean the outside of cup and plate* (Mt 23:25–26). There were special observances for the washing of these things. The Pharisees observed all the external requirements of their religion while remaining grasping and wicked.

41. *Give alms from what you have . . .* This verse is generally recognised as obscure, but the meaning seems to be that if the heart is right, then religious practices will have an end beyond themselves.

11:42. *You who pay your tithe of mint and rue.* A tithe (one-tenth) of a man's property was given to the Temple as due to God. Garden herbs were excepted as being too trivial but many Pharisees tithed them all the same.

> *And overlook justice and the love of God.*
> 'This is what Yahweh asks of you
> only this, to act justly
> to love tenderly
> and to walk humbly with your God'
> (Micah 6:7–8)

44. *You are like the unmarked tombs* (Mt 23:27). People incurred religious defilement by walking over these. The Pharisees, by concealing their true character, misled everyone.

45. *A lawyer then spoke.* Lk preferred to call them lawyers because they were entirely concerned with the interpretation of the Law. 'Scribe' would have meant 'clerk' or 'secretary' to his gentile readers.

46. *You load on men burdens* (Intro B 2.3). It was said that if a single person could keep all the sabbath regulations without a fault, the kingdom of God would come at once. There were so many, however, that nobody could, and there was only stern rebuke for failure to keep the Law.

47. *You who build the tombs of the prophets.* The prophets insisted on the importance of care for others as basic to true religion, but all the lawyers cared about was the ceremonial observance enjoined by the Law. These were as useful as elaborate tombs when it was a man's teaching or message which really kept his memory alive. Their ancestors killed the prophets, and the contemporaries of Jesus themselves ensured that their message was overlaid with what was unimportant.

49. *The Wisdom of God*, or perhaps 'God in his wisdom'.

161

The words appear to be followed by a quotation, but from what source is not known. Neither Abel (Genesis 4:2–9) nor Zechariah (II Chronicles 24:22) were prophets.

11:52. *The key of knowledge*, i.e. the knowledge of God, not an intellectual knowledge about Him, but experience as of a person. By their methods of interpretation, the lawyers had obscured the simple truths of the Scriptures.

Open and fearless speech

12:1. *The yeast of the Pharisees . . . hypocrisy*. It was the lawyers who had developed the ceremonial system; it was the Pharisees who deceived themselves and other people, putting it into practice (3:8; 5:29–32; 7:36–50; 11:42).

2. *Everything will be uncovered*. This seems to be a warning to the Pharisees. Eventually they will be unmasked.

3. *What you have said in the dark . . .* The truth will come out, and be openly proclaimed.

4. *Those who kill the body*. Death was the punishment for refusing to worship the emperor after the fall of Jerusalem, in the second half of the first century.

5. *Fear him who . . . has power to cast into hell*. Those who weakened under persecution, denied God and worshipped the gods, would have to face the judgement of God.

6. *Five sparrows*. The cheapest life in the market. The fear of God is to be balanced by love of the heavenly Father who cares for His most insignificant creatures, and holds Christ's disciples most precious.

10. *Everyone who says a word against the Son of Man . . .* As it stands this seems to contradict what has been said vv. 8–9. Reference to Mk 3:28 suggests that at

162

some stage there has been a copyist's error, and that in Mk we have the correct form of the saying.

Blasphemy against the Holy Spirit. No single, specific sin is meant here; but the love of and indulgence in all evil in preference to what is good and true.

12:11. *When they take you before synagogues.* The elders of the synagogue were responsible for the members of the congregation, and could sentence them to 39 strokes of the rod for offences considered serious. St Paul was punished five times in this way. As far as we know, the disciples had no experiences of this kind until after Pentecost.

On hoarding possessions

13. *Master, tell my brother.* A teacher was the natural person to give help, but as always Jesus would not give judgement on the particular question brought to him. Instead he gave a general principle as a guide, as in the situation which produced the parable of the good Samaritan (10:29f.).

15. *A man's life is not made secure by what he owns.* Possessions should never be a cause of quarrel between brothers. Relationships are more important than things or wealth.

20. *This hoard of yours, whose will it be?* You leave your material wealth behind you at death, and therefore it is only sense to regard it as of only secondary importance now.

Trust in Providence (Mt 6:25–34)

On almsgiving (Mt 6:19–21)

On being ready for the Master's return

After Peter's profession of faith (9:26–27) there is the first mention of the Son of Man coming in glory, and of the shortness of the time before the establishment of the kingdom. The subject is now developed. The language of crisis and the nearness of the end is foreign to modern thinking. But the Church came to understand it in terms of human experience: to most people there comes a moment of choice between continuance in the faith and departure from it, not the less critical because the definiteness of the choice involved is often obscured.

12:35. *Dressed for action . . . lamps lit.* The crisis is so close that the disciples must be ready at any moment. No one knows when or how his test will arise.

Two parables about preparedness now follow:
(i) *The master returning from the wedding feast*

36. The wedding feast here is not the Messianic banquet since the master is returning from it. The story has been altered in the course of transmission.

37. *He will sit them down at table and wait on them.* The procedure is highly improbable, but this is the banquet at which the obedient find places and joy beyond all expectation.

38. *The second watch.* The Jews divided the night into three periods, the Romans into four.

(ii) *The burglar*

39. The walls of the houses were of clay and easy to penetrate. In parts of the Middle East, thieves still use the same technique.

42. *What sort of steward then is faithful?* The landowners left the organisation and control of their estates in the hands of stewards. These men owed absolute obedience to their masters, and on the other hand had unchallenged authority over the slaves and free labourers who did all the work.

43. *Happy that servant . . .* Happiness is the outcome of faithful service the reward of which is greater responsibility, not greater ease (19:11–26).

12:48. *When a man has a great deal given him . . .* The disciples had been taught what Christ expected of them and therefore must be ready to shoulder great responsibilities.

Jesus and his Passion

49. *I have come to bring fire to the earth.* Jesus lifted up upon the cross was going to be a blazing beacon, a challenge for ever to the belief that wealth, force, and self-interest achieve anything of lasting value.

50. *There is a baptism I must receive.* Being overwhelmed by deep waters is an Old Testament metaphor for suffering, and at his baptism by John, Jesus had begun his public ministry which was to end in his death. He was the suffering Messiah.

Jesus the cause of dissension

There can be no compromise about the Crucified Christ; there is no middle way between acceptance and rejection (11:23).

On reading the signs of the times

56. *You do not know how to interpret these times.* Jesus himself was sufficient sign (11:29–32).

58. *When you go to court with your opponent.* The debtor symbolising the sinner, is represented as coming to an agreement with the creditor on the way to the law court, in the hope of escaping deserved punishment. Israel is in just such a situation. If the Chosen People fail in this time of crisis, the penalty will be terrible.

59. *The very last penny.* The siege of Jerusalem in 70 and the end of nationalist hopes is probably to be inferred.

The people were at fault in religious matters because they put observance of the Law first, overlooking considerations of justice and compassion: they were at fault politically because they cherished hopes of a Messiah who would drive out the Romans, give world dominion to the Jews, and make Jerusalem the capital of the world. Destruction of the people was inevitable unless they 'repented', unless they abandoned these false desires and came to understand Jesus as the Way, the Truth, and the Life.

13 **Examples inviting repentance**

Two examples of sudden and totally unexpected disaster are given. Israel would be taken unawares in just the same way and there was no time to lose in responding to Jesus and accepting the Gospel. The situation was one of crisis (12:35–40).

1. *The Galileans.* Nothing is known from other sources of this episode but Pilate had a reputation for brutality, and the slaughter of Galileans who had come to Jerusalem to offer sacrifice is in character.

4. *The tower at Siloam.* Pilate provided the city with a better water supply, paid for out of Temple funds. The accident may have happened while the aqueduct was being constructed.
Do you think that they were more guilty . . . ? The Jews believed that adversity of all kinds was God's punishment for sin.

5. *You will all perish as they did,* i.e. unexpectedly (12:35–40).

Parable of the barren fig tree

The fig tree is the symbol for Israel, the fruit representing the obedience which God expected from His people.

7. *For three years.* This may be a reference to a three-year ministry of Jesus, but should more probably be

166

understood as the whole period of Israel's preparation for the supreme moment of her history.

Cut it down. Israel was on the brink of destruction.

13:8. *Leave it one more year.* Jesus was patient and merciful, showing mankind the character of God the Father.

Healing of the crippled woman on the sabbath

The story illustrates the attitude of Jesus to the legalism of the religious authorities, as also 6:6–11. It has been introduced at this point because the woman, a daughter of Abraham (a Jew) being possessed by a spirit, typifies the different kinds of outcasts from Jewish society. The repentance of Israel which is such an urgent necessity, will best be demonstrated by a generous attitude to these people.

Parable of the mustard seed (Mk 4:31–32; Mt 13:31–32)

18. *The kingdom of God* (6:20–49; 8:4–15; 9:26–27)

There are two points to notice in this comparison. (i) The tiny seed became a tree: the insignificant beginning is contrasted with the richness of the final development, when the gentile nations (the birds of the air) are included within the kingdom. (ii) The process of growth, once begun, cannot be halted but must continue.

Parable of the yeast (Mt 13:33)

The meaning is the same as that of the parable of the mustard seed with the additional idea of the permeating action of the leaven: the members of the kingdom will affect manners and customs, making them good.

The two parables emphasise the fact that no amount of opposition to Jesus can stop the coming of the kingdom, and so underline the urgent need for a change of heart (repentance) in Israel.

The narrow door; rejection of the Jews, call of the gentiles

13:23. *Will there be only a few saved?* This was a common subject of discussion, showing how harsh was the general idea of God.

24. *Try your best.* Obedience is rooted in humility and requires self-discipline.
The narrow door. Perhaps Jesus was thinking particularly of the demands of love (6:27), and compassion (10:30–37).

25. *The master . . . locked the door.* God does not want to exclude anyone from the kingdom. People exclude themselves by deliberately preferring evil, and shutting their eyes to the needs of others (Mt 25:31–46).

29. *The feast.* The Messianic banquet (9:16). It would be crowded with gentiles while the Chosen People remained outside.

30. *Those now last who will be first* (Mk 10:31; Mt 19:30; 20:16). The gentiles will rank before Israel.

Herod the fox

It is interesting that the Pharisees came with a friendly warning, unless they were really messengers from Herod who wanted to rid his territory of the presence of Jesus by a threat.

31. *Herod.* Herod Antipas, ruler of Galilee.

32. *Today and tomorrow . . . and on the third day.* Jesus would continue with his mighty works for a short and definite period to be decided by himself and without any reference to Herod.
On the third day attain my end. In the older versions 'I am perfected', a reference to the Passion, resurrection, and ascension of Jesus to the Father in heaven.

Jerusalem admonished (Mt 23:37–39)

13:34. *Jerusalem, you that kill the prophets.* The city is perhaps to be understood as representing Israel as a whole since there is nothing in the Old Testament to indicate that many prophets met their death there.

35. *Your house will be left to you.* A prophecy of the destruction of Jerusalem and the Temple which was always called 'God's house'. Perhaps it is described here as 'your house' because God will withdraw His presence from it (Mt 23:29).
You shall not see me until the time comes . . . The allusion is probably to the final coming of Christ in triumph (21:27).
Blessings on him who comes . . . (Psalm 118:26), sung at Passover and used by the crowds when Jesus rode in triumph into Jerusalem before his arrest and crucifixion (19:38).

14 **Healing of a dropsical man on the sabbath** (Lk only) (6:6–11; 13:10–17)

On choosing places at table (Mt 23:6)

Arrogance was a fault of the Pharisees as well as legalism, but behind the reproof about their social behaviour lies condemnation of their conviction that good places in the kingdom of God were theirs by right (3:8).

The invited guests who made excuses

16. *A man gave a great banquet.* God prepared the Messianic feast.

17. *His servant.* Jesus.
Those invited. The Jews: they had no one to blame but themselves for their exclusion from the kingdom.

21. *Go out quickly into the streets and alleys of the town.*

The outcasts were invited to take the places of the Jews.

14:23. *Go to the open roads and hedgerows.* People from outside the city were then called, the gentiles.

Renouncing all that one holds dear

26. *Without hating . . . he cannot be my disciple.* The word translated 'hate' means only 'to put in second place'; God must come first in a man's life (9:60).

Renouncing possessions

Two parables follow to teach that discipleship is not to be embarked upon in a momentary burst of feeling, but only after deliberate calculation of the cost.

28. *Which of you intending to build a tower . . . ?* It was a farm building of some kind (Mk 12:1). Any sensible person gets an estimate before starting an important project.

31. *The king . . . ten thousand . . . twenty thousand.* The disciple is always at what appears a disadvantage from a worldly point of view because he cannot fight God's battles with worldly weapons, and must decide if he can endure poverty, hardship, and persecution.

33. *He gives up all his possessions.* The disciple must be ready to risk all for Christ and not cling to what he owns, position and authority as well as goods.

The three parables of God's mercy

15 The situation in which the parables were told is important. They were aimed at the Pharisees.

The lost sheep (Mt 18:12–14)

Notice particularly the tirelessness of the search, the value set on the individual gone astray, and the joy at its recovery; Christ is describing the care and concern of the heavenly Father.

15:7. *Ninety-nine virtuous men.* This is irony; the self-satisfaction of the Pharisees blinded them to their grave sins, cruelty and injustice.

The lost drachma (Lk only)

The houses of the poor were very dark, and the drachma (a small coin) was very precious and part of the dowry. The parable repeats the lesson of the previous one.

The lost son ('the prodigal') and the dutiful son (Lk only)

13. *The younger son.* He represents the 'sinners', the outcasts.

15. *He hired himself . . . to feed the pigs.* Pigs were regarded as unclean by the Jews, so this detail shows the degree to which he was outcast.

18. *I have sinned against heaven and against you.* He was quite honest about his own conduct.

19. *Treat me as one of your paid servants.* He could not undo the past, but he would make up as far as he could for what he had done.

20. *While he was still a long way off, his father . . . ran to the boy.* God wants His straying children back, and in His mercy goes out at speed to meet them and bring them home as they stumble towards Him.

22. *The best robe . . . a ring . . . sandals.* These things represent the completeness of the young man's restoration to the status of son, the past forgotten. The episode illustrates exactly what is meant by forgiveness.

The parables had a particular application to the people who first heard them, the Pharisees being rebuked for their contempt of their fellow men, but the teaching is fundamental for Christians everywhere. (i) God cares for every individual. (ii) He is active in bringing each one back. (iii) He can restore the people who have left Him to follow their own devices.

15:25. *The elder brother*. This man typifies the Pharisees and scribes, and respectable people everywhere. There must be no jealousy or suspicion of the restored sinner, only welcome and joy at his return.

16　**The crafty steward** (Lk only)
This parable must be taken simply as a story with a moral which is to be found in v. 8. The rich man and the steward do not represent God and the Pharisees respectively.

1. *The steward*. For his functions see 12:42. He had been wasteful but not necessarily fraudulent.

5. *He called his master's debtors*. When he knew that there was to be an audit, he proceeded to falsify the accounts with the help of the debtors. On the one hand the books would not look so bad, and on the other the debtors would not forget that he had done them a good turn and would befriend him.

8. *The master praised the dishonest steward*. Not because he had been dishonest but because he had been clever. *The children of light*. Religious people generally and the Pharisees in particular, would do well to be equally clever in making friends, not for their own advantage but to bring them into the kingdom of God.

The right use of money

9. *Use money tainted as it is*. It is not clear why money is tainted—perhaps because it is a temptation—but it is to be used to win friends.
When it fails you. After this life when it is of no use. (On hoarding possessions 12:13–21.)

They will welcome you. This probably means 'God will welcome you'. The scribes often used the verb in the third person plural to avoid using the divine name, and it may be the case here. Then 'the friends' v. 9 also signify God, and the general sense of the saying is that money is to be used in a way that will please God.

16:11. *Genuine riches.* Worldly wealth is contrasted with spiritual treasure. Trustworthy service in what is external, like money, will be rewarded with larger opportunities of serving God.

The kingdom stormed

16. *Up to the time of John.* John the Baptist was the link between the old religion of the Law and the Prophets, and the new religion of the Gospel.
By violence everyone is getting in. Men were reckoning the cost of discipleship (14:28–33) and renouncing all to follow Christ.

The Law remains (Mt 5:18)

17. *One little stroke.* This was probably a small decoration used by the scribes above certain letters in the Hebrew Scriptures. Jesus is saying that it is easier for heaven and earth to disappear than for the scribes to give up the smallest bit of the ritual law by which they hid the real demands of God's Law. Mt 5:18 is best understood as the revision of the original saying by a scribe who had become a Christian and failed to see our Lord's point.

Marriage indissoluble (Mk 10:11–12; Mt 5:31–32; 19:9)

The ruling of Jesus on this matter was stricter than that of the scribe Shammai who allowed divorce only in the case of adultery by the wife: under Jewish Law the wife had no rights and could not divorce her husband, while the man could be held to have committed adultery only against a husband he had wronged but not against his own wife. Lk and Mk agree in saying (i) Jesus allowed no grounds for divorce at all, and (ii) put the husband on an equality with his wife by pronouncing him guilty of adultery against her if he was unfaithful.

The rich man and Lazarus

16:19. *A rich man.* The description of his dress suggests that he was a Sadducee (Intro B 1). The royal purple and the fine linen, the richest material available, are typical.

20. *A poor man called Lazarus.* A fictitious character and the only person in the parables of Jesus to be named.

22. *The bosom of Abraham.* A Jewish figure of speech. Lazarus the outcast, went to heaven where he enjoyed the company of the fathers of the Jewish race.
The rich man also died and was buried. That should have been the end of everything according to his way of thinking.

23. *Hades.* A shadowy abode of the dead.

24. *I am in agony in these flames.* Jesus was not providing factual information about the conditions of existence after death. Using imagery familiar to his hearers from Jewish literature, he was driving home the vital importance of concern about material conditions as an element in discipleship, as in Ch. 15 mercy and understanding for people unacceptable on moral grounds was urged.

27. *Send Lazarus to my Father's house.* The rich man was becoming capable of thinking of other people.

29. *They have Moses and the prophets.* The Scriptures teach the belief which the Sadducees rejected.

30. *Even if someone should rise from the dead.* A reference to the resurrection.

Our Lord seems here to have adapted to his use a folk tale that circulated in first-century Palestine, and which may have originated in Egypt since a very similar story is found there. He teaches (i) that there is a future life; (ii) Right belief on this point affects conduct here and now.

On leading others astray (Mt 18:6–7; Mk 9:42)

17:1. *Obstacles*. Positive false teaching is probably meant.

2. *These little ones*. Adult converts not yet grown strong in the faith, rather than children in the literal sense.

Brotherly correction (Mt 18:21–22)

4. *Seven times*. The figure is used in the Bible to represent completeness and should never be understood literally. There is to be no limit to the number of times that the penitent is to be forgiven (Mt 18:23–35).

The power of faith

5. *Increase our faith.* The apostle saw that much faith was needed if they were to be able always to forgive.

6. *You could say to this mulberry tree* . . . Mulberry trees are very deep rooted, a point which adds to the absurdity of the project envisaged. The words are not to be taken literally and mean that by faith in Christ, the disciples can accomplish the seemingly impossible in his service.

Humble service

7. *Which of you, with a servant* . . . The disciple as the servant of God, must never think that he has done enough to seek out and help the weak and the lost (9:23).

10. *We are merely servants*. God has brought us into existence and therefore our commitment to Him must be total.

The ten lepers

17:14. *Go and show yourselves to the priests* (5:14).

16. *The man was a Samaritan* (9:52; 10:30f.).

19. *Your faith has saved you* (7:9, 50; 8:25; 9:41).

The coming of the kingdom of God

20. *Asked . . . when the kingdom of God was to come.* The Pharisees thought it was still in the future.

21. *The kingdom of God is among you.* The kingdom of God had started, a process which could not be halted but must go on to full development (13:18–21).

The day of the Son of Man

22. *One of the days of the Son of Man.* The Parousia, the return of Christ in power (9:26–27).

23. *They will say . . .* i.e. False prophets and false messiahs (Mk 13:21–23).

24. *The lightning.* The brilliance of the coming will accentuate the darkness of the world.

26. *As it was in Noah's day* (Genesis chs. 6–8). The people were going about their ordinary business when they were suddenly overtaken by catastrophe. The second example of Lot was given to emphasise the point that the Parousia would be totally unexpected.

31. *When that day comes . . .* Possibly this saying originally referred to the destruction of Jerusalem, an event which Jesus is recorded elsewhere as prophesying, and in the process of transmission it was confused with the Parousia which it prefigured.

35. *One will be taken, the other left.* The coming of the Son of Man separates mankind into two divisions (12:51–53).

37. *Where, Lord?* Earlier, v. 20, the Pharisees had wanted to know when the kingdom of God was to come; the

disciples now inquire as to its whereabouts. To neither question would Jesus give an answer (Mk 13:32).

Where the body is . . . This is probably a proverbial saying, used to convey two ideas. (i) The Parousia is as inevitable as the fate of anything that dies in the wilderness. (ii) It will be swift like the vultures which swoop upon their prey.

The unscrupulous judge and the importunate widow (Lk only)

18 For other teaching on prayer, 11:1–13.

3. *There was a widow.* The type of defencelessness and desolation (7:11–17).

5. *Since she keeps pestering me* . . . The same point appears to be made as in the parable of the importunate friend (11:8). Persistence will be enough.

7. *Will not God see justice done* . . . *?* The contrast in character between the unjust judge and God the Father who cares for those who cry to Him, is the basic lesson of the parable. Tireless prayer can be offered in the sure confidence that He hears. He is utterly dependable. It is a message of hope to those who suffer oppression and injustice.

The Pharisee and the publican (tax collector) (Lk only)

This parable deals with the attitude of the worshipper in his approach to God, and is therefore a companion to the previous one with its emphasis on the character of God.

11. *The Pharisee stood there and said this prayer to himself.* Standing was the usual position in prayer. The man was not only complacent, but he relied on himself for his achievements and not on God. Contrast the words of Christ to St Paul (II Cor. 12:9–10), 'My grace is enough for you; my power is at its best in weakness.'

18:12. *I fast twice a week* ... One fast a week was all that the Law really required, and it was not necessary to give tithes on everything. He did these things for his own honour and glory, rather than for God (11:38–44).

13. *The tax collector*. The man was a shady character, and he knew it. But because he was humble and recognised himself for what he was, he was capable of growth, and entry into the kingdom of God, like the prodigal son (15:11–32).

Lk has nearly finished his account of the journey up to Jerusalem (IV. 9:51), and at this point picks up Mk's narrative (Mk 10:13f).

Jesus and the children

16. *It is to such as these that the kingdom of God belongs*. Simplicity and trust were probably the childlike qualities that Jesus had in mind, something very different from the calculating attitude of the Pharisee in the parable.

The rich aristocrat (Mk 10:17–22; Mt 19:16–22)

18. *Eternal life*. Quality of life; life with God (10:25).

20. *You know the commandments* (Exodus 20:12–16). The man had found that just keeping the commandments which he had perhaps never wanted to break, was not enough, or he would not have asked his question.

22. *Sell all that you own and distribute the money*. For other passages giving the teaching of Jesus on wealth 12:13–21, 33–34.
Follow me. Eternal life could only be inherited by getting rid of what rivalled the claims of God, in this case wealth, and entering into a personal relationship with Jesus.

The reward of renunciation

This is the climax of our Lord's teaching on disciple-

ship. (i) 9:23–24. It was shown to be a costly participation in the creative suffering of Christ. (ii) 14:25–33.
So much was involved in it that careful consideration
must be given before entering upon it. Now (iii)
18:28–30 the reward is shown to be beyond all calculation. The parables of the treasure and the pearl
(Mt 13:44–46) convey the same teaching.

Third prophecy of the Passion (9:22, 44)

18:31. *Everything that is written by the prophets* . . . Lk often
remarks that the Passion was foretold by the prophets
(24:25, 27, 44; Servant Songs 3:22).

   34. *They had no idea what he meant.* The disciples were
spiritually blind. Their condition was reflected in the
physical blindness of the man in Jericho, in the next
story.

Entering Jericho: the blind man

   38. *Son of David* (5:24). Jesus quietly accepted the title.
He would shortly ride into Jerusalem as Messiah.

   42. *Your faith has saved you.* Lk probably had in mind
that the spiritual blindness of the disciples (v. 34)
would be cured.

Zacchaeus (Lk only)

19:1. *Jericho.* Like Capernaum (4:31; 5:27) Jericho was an
important customs post.

   7. *They all complained.* The crowd, not only the religious
leaders.

   8. *I am going to give half my property* . . . In his plan for
restitution, Zacchaeus did far more than the Law
required.

   9. *This man too is a son of Abraham* (3:8). The response
of Zacchaeus to Jesus was in marked contrast to that
of the young aristocrat (18:18–23).

19:10. *The Son of Man has come to seek out and save* . . . The words recall the parables ch. 15.

Parable of the pounds

11. *He was near Jerusalem.* At Jericho Jesus had been saluted as Son of David, Messiah, and the crowds were getting excited because they expected the kingdom to be established on arrival at Jerusalem. The parable teaches (i) that the kingdom will not be established immediately, and (ii) that when it does come it will not be political in character but will take the form of Final Judgement.

    The parable of the talents (Mt 25:14–30) is probably another version of an original which became modified in the process of transmission. Additional matter in Lk seems to be derived from a historical event. After the death of Herod the Great (Intro B) his eldest son, Archelaus, went to Rome to have his position as king confirmed, but was so much hated that a delegation went from Jerusalem to try to prevent the appointment.

12. *A man of noble birth went to a distant country.* Christ went to heaven to receive a kingdom. The parable is concerned with the period after the ascension (24:50).

13. *He summoned ten servants.* Ten was often used as a round number, so these are not the apostles but Christians in general who are expected to act for Christ during his absence.

14. *His compatriots detested him.* The Jews rejected him.

15. *On his return.* At the Parousia, the Second Coming.
    He sent for those servants. At the Last Judgement every man has to render an account.

17. *Faithful in a very small thing.* . . . The reward for faithful service is not more ease but more responsibility.

19:20. *I put it away safely in a piece of linen.* In Mt's version the bad servant hid his talent in the ground.

22. *You knew I was an exacting man* (17:7–10).

24. *Take the pound from him.* If gifts that could be used for God's service are not exercised and opportunities neglected, others will step in and then there will be no more opportunities.

27. *As for my enemies . . . execute them.* This sounds like Archelaus not our Lord, but it finds a place in the parable because Lk like all other members of the early Church, believed that the acceptance or rejection of Jesus was like the difference between life and death (11:23).

The story is to be understood as an allegory of the Christian life between the ascension and the Parousia and should be considered in connection with the teaching on discipleship (18:28).

V. THE JERUSALEM MINISTRY

The Messiah enters Jerusalem (Mk 11:1–11; Mt 21: 1–11; Jn 12:12–16)

Prophets of the Old Testament sometimes used symbolic acts in order to drive home some particular message; mimes we might call them (I Kings 11:29–40; Jeremiah 19:1–13). The entry was such an act.

29. *Bethphage and Bethany, close by the Mount of Olives.* The Mount of Olives is just outside Jerusalem, a very steep hill rather than a mountain. Bethany was the home of Martha and Mary (10:38–42). Bethphage was not a village at all but just a stretch of the mountain.

32. *The messengers . . . found everything just as he had told them.* It had all been prearranged and there was a password to guard against any mistake.

181

19:35. *They took the colt to Jesus.* It was an ass's colt (Mt 21:2; Jn 12:15), the royal mount of the king coming in peace. Unlike Mt and Jn, Lk makes no mention of the prophecy, Zechariah 9:9.

36. *People spread their cloaks in the road.* Lk makes no mention of greenery strewn before the colt, unlike the other evangelists.

37. *The whole group of the disciples.* It was obligatory for all Jews to be in Jerusalem for Passover, so the road must have been thronged with pilgrims.

38. *Blessings on the King who comes.* This is from the special Passover Psalm 118:26 which sprang naturally to mind.
Peace in heaven. The song of the angels (2:14).

Jesus defends his disciples for acclaiming him (Lk only)

Lk records the protest of the Pharisees while in Mt it was the chief priests and scribes who were indignant at the expulsion of the dealers from the Temple (Mt 21:12–17). Both groups tried to discredit Jesus in the eyes of the people during the next few days.

Lament for Jerusalem (Lk only)

41. *As he drew near.* From the slopes of the Mount of Olives you look down on Jerusalem and have a wonderful view of the city.

42. *The message of peace.* The people of Jerusalem were militant nationalists and rejected the peace which Jesus offered.

43. *Your enemies will raise fortifications all around you.* A prophecy of the siege of Jerusalem in 70 (Intro B).

44. *All because you did not recognise your opportunity.* The rejection of Jesus was decisive in the history of the people (11:29–32).

The expulsion of the dealers from the Temple (Mk 11: 15–19; Mt 21:12–17)

Lk gives the barest statement about this episode, probably because he was writing after the destruction of the Temple, and for gentiles who had never thought of it as their place of prayer.

The Jews question the authority of Jesus

20:2. *What authority have you for acting like this?* The chief priests were angry because Jesus had driven the dealers out of the Temple for which they were responsible. The scribes were angry because he taught as having authority himself without reference to the traditions (Intro B 3).

4. *John's baptism: did it come from heaven, or from man?* It was a double-edged question. Not only would the people be infuriated if they said the baptism came from man. If they said it came from heaven, they would have to recognise Jesus who was marked out as Messiah by John's baptism.

The parable of the wicked husbandmen

This provides the answer to the question on authority, above.

9. *A man planted a vineyard.* The vineyard is the Old Testament symbol for the Israel of God. The man therefore represents God, and the tenants succeeding generations of Jews.

10. *He sent a servant to the tenants.* The servants sent by God were the prophets; the produce or fruit (13:7) represents the obedient service due to God.

11. *The tenants thrashed* (*them*). The prophets were always disregarded and roughly handled (13:34; 11:50–51).

13. *I will send them my dear son.* Finally God sent His Son, Jesus Christ, but they plotted to kill him.

20 :15. *They threw him out of the vineyard.* The Law (Deuteronomy 21:22–23) says that a man 'hanged on a tree' (crucified) is 'accursed of God'. Thus Jesus the Son of God in whom the destiny of Israel came to a climax, would be held accursed, excommunicated from the people of God.

16. *He will come and make an end of these tenants.* The Jewish nation ceased to exist after the destruction of Jerusalem in 70.
    He will . . . give the vineyard to others. The old Israel would be replaced by the new Israel, the disciples of Christ. By the time this gospel was written, the gentiles in the Church far outnumbered the people of Jewish extraction.

17. *It was the stone rejected by the builders. . . .* (Psalm 118:22.) The first Christians collected Old Testament texts, now called 'proof texts', which they thought related to particular aspects of the life and Passion of our Lord. This one they interpreted as a prophecy of his rejection, and the consequences.

On tribute to Caesar

20. *They . . . sent agents.* Mk says it was the Pharisees and Herodians who tried to trap Jesus with this question (Mk 12:13–17). In Lk it was agents sent by the chief priests.

22. *Is it permissible for us to pay taxes to Caesar?* It was a burning question among all Jews at that time. They detested the Roman coinage in which the tax was paid, both because it was a sign of their subjugation and because it was stamped with the name and head of Caesar, a breach of the commandment not to make a carved image or likeness of anything.

25. *Give back to Caesar what belongs to Caesar.* In the centuries during which the Church grew within the heathen Empire, this saying of Jesus was a very impor-

tant and practical directive. Whether heathen or not, the state needs funds to provide for its citizens and all should contribute. St Paul saw to it that his converts knew their duty in this matter (Romans 13:1–7).

The resurrection of the dead

20:27. *Some Sadducees* (Intro B 1) (16:19–31)

28. *We have it from Moses . . .* Moses was held to be the author of Deuteronomy, the book of the Law. The situation described by the Sadducees was known as levirate marriage (Deut. 25:5–6). It was a way of providing for widows who would otherwise be destitute, as well as of producing children to keep green the memory of the dead.

34. *The children of this world.* A Hebrew way of saying 'People'.

35. *Those who are judged worthy of a place . . .* Lk did not think that everyone attained the resurrection life (Mk 12:25–27).
They . . . do not marry because they can no longer die. They have no longer need of children to see they are not forgotten.

36. *Children of the resurrection . . . sons of God.* Belief in resurrection stems from belief in the reality of the relationship with God begun in this life.

37. *Moses himself implies . . .* (Exodus 3:1–6). The Sadducees prided themselves on not believing any doctrine not found in the Scriptures and it is important therefore that Jesus used the Scriptures to show them their error.

Christ, not only son but also Lord of David

42. *The Lord said to my Lord . . .* (Psalm 110:1), another of the proof texts (v. 17) of the early Church.

21 In 17:22–37, following one of his sources, Lk speaks of the coming of Jesus in glory at the end of time. In

this chapter he follows Mk 13 where two groups of ideas merge, the final coming and the destruction of Jerusalem.

21:5. *Some were talking about the Temple.* Herod the Great began its reconstruction on a lavish scale about 20 B.C., and it was not completed until about A.D. 63 only a few years before it was totally destroyed.

The warning signs

8. *Many will come using my name.* People who claim to be the Christ.

15. *I myself will give you eloquence.* Lk 12:12, 'The Holy Spirit will teach you what you must say.' Mt 10:20, 'The Spirit of your Father will be speaking in you.' The experience of Christians went ahead of the formulation of doctrine, and St Paul writes interchangeably of the Spirit of Jesus and the Holy Spirit.

The siege (17:31)
Disaster and the age of the pagans

24. *The age of the pagans.* i.e. The period during which the pagans will take the place of the unfaithful Jewish nation. St Paul sees this as ending with the conversion of all Israel (Romans 11:11–32).

The time of this coming

28. *When you see these things . . . the kingdom of God is near.* The kingdom has already come (9:27; 17:21), but the reference here is to its triumphant progress which will begin with the destruction of Jerusalem.

APOCALYPTIC LITERATURE

In the 2nd century B.C. at a time of national disaster a type of literature appeared which was designed to comfort the faithful and persecuted remnant of the people. It described how, after a series of disasters and signs in heaven, God would intervene and His reign would be established. It is called 'apocalyptic' from a Greek word meaning 'to unveil', the authors imagining angels as revealing to some human inquirer what the future course of history would be. 21:5–28 is apocalyptic in character, and it is a great mistake as people have so often done, to try to identify events contemporary with themselves with the particular details of any apocalyptic work. The chief value of this type of literature lies in its insistence on the fact that God will triumph over evil in all its forms, and in its command to be continually on the alert. The Book of Revelation, the last book in the New Testament, is the best-known work of this kind.

VI. THE PASSION

The conspiracy against Jesus: Judas betrays him

22:1. *The feast of Unleavened Bread, called the Passover.* It is important to remember that the Passover is the feast which commemorates the salvation of the Israelites by God when they escaped from Egypt (Exodus 12). Jn, by making it clear that Jesus was dying on the cross at the time when the Passover lambs were being slain, shows how the first Christians—Jews born and bred—understood the self-offering of Jesus as effecting perfectly what the earlier salvation commemorated in the Passover, only foreshadowed; (i) salvation from sin, not merely physical salvation; (ii) union of the people with God and with one another. Lk thought along the same lines. Originally the feast of Unleavened Bread came after the Passover but in the gospels they appear to be identified. Leaven was the symbol of impurity and so the unleavened bread typified the people of God, cleansed from sin.

Lk makes no mention of the anointing at Bethany (Mk 14:3–9; Mt 26:6–13; Jn 12:1–8) possibly because he has described an anointing early in the ministry (7:36–50).

22:3. *Satan entered into Judas.* Jn 13:27 describes it in the same way. The idea that Judas betrayed Jesus out of greed for money derives from Mt's story of the thirty pieces of silver (Mt 26:14–16) and Jn's statement that he was a thief (Jn 12:4–6).

   4. *Officers of the guard.* Temple police under the control of the priests. They were of course Jews and independent of the Roman Governor.

Preparation for the Passover supper (Mk 14:12–16)

Lk follows Mk closely in this section but names the two disciples sent ahead as Peter and John. As in the case of the entry into Jerusalem arrangements had been made in advance (19:29–40).

 10. *A man carrying a pitcher of water.* He would be conspicuous because it was generally women who got the water.

 12. *A large upper room.* The inhabitants of Jerusalem expected to give hospitality to pilgrims at Passover when people thronged into the city.

The supper

 14. *When the hour was come.* This is like the language of Jn where 'the hour' always suggests the suffering and death of Jesus.

 15. *I have longed to eat this passover with you.* The bread and the cup (v. 17) were essential parts of the passover meal. Lk was making clear the parallel between the

old rite of the Jewish Passover and the new rite of the Christian Eucharist (Holy Communion).

22:16. *Until it is fulfilled in the kingdom of God.* The Passover was a first stage; the Eucharist is the second stage, the centre of spiritual life in the kingdom for us now; the Messianic banquet at the end of time is the final stage (v. 30).

The institution of the Eucharist

'Eucharist' is a word derived from the Greek and means 'Thanksgiving', thanksgiving for the salvation made available to all men by Christ. The word was used from the first for Holy Communion. Vv. 19–20 should be compared with I Corinthians 11:24–25, St Paul's being the earliest account of the Eucharist which has come down to us.

19. *He took some bread.* The actions of Jesus were the usual ones of a Jewish host, as in the miracle of the loaves. He took, gave thanks, broke and gave.
This is my body. The words were startling. Bread is the staple food of simple people, the commonest thing. Jesus took our ordinary humanity. He consecrated it to the service of the Father; the breaking is a reminder of his suffering and death, the cost of our salvation; the giving is the gift of himself, his grace and power (II Corinthians 12:9).
Do this as a memorial to me. The disciples were to continue to do this not merely as a reminder of a person who had gone, but as the means whereby he would be known by succeeding generations.

20. *This cup is the new covenant in my blood.* When the tribes of Israel reached Mt Sinai after their escape from Egypt under the leadership of Moses, they were given the Law. If they promised obedience to God they would be His people, a kingdom of priests, a consecrated nation. The people accordingly promised

obedience (Exodus 19:3–8) and the covenant or agreement between God and the people was confirmed by a sacrifice (Exodus 24:1–8). Bullocks were slain and and offered, half the blood being cast on the altar and half on the people. It was the ancient belief that life was in the blood and this use of the blood, therefore, was regarded as binding parties to a covenant, in this case God and the Israelites, in a common life.

The prophets in the following centuries thundered against the Chosen People for their disobedience, and at last Jeremiah said that the time would come when God would give a new covenant to His people (Jeremiah 31:31–34). Now at the supper Jesus gave the new covenant which would be sealed by his blood, and called the cup of wine the new covenant in his blood.

The treachery of Judas foretold

In Mk this prediction is placed before the institution of the Eucharist (Mk 14:18–21).

Who is the greatest?

The question had already risen 9:46–48. Only Lk mentions the dispute as having occurred at the supper.

22:25. *The title Benefactor*. This was a complimentary title often given to kings at that time.

27. *Here am I among you as one who serves* (Jn 13:1–11). The disciple is to follow as best he can the example of Christ, the Eucharist being a continual reminder of what is involved (18:22).

The reward promised to the apostles (Lk only)

30. *You will eat and drink at my table in my kingdom*. The Messianic banquet (v. 16). The Psalms provide an insight to the significance of the imagery. There is 'unbounded joy' in the presence of God (Ps 16:11).

God alone can feast the soul (Ps 63:5), and satisfy hunger (Ps 107:9).

You will sit on thrones to judge. The apostles would witness to the fact of the resurrection to all the nations in the power of the Holy Spirit (Acts 1:8) and exercise authority over the new Israel.

Peter's denial and repentance foretold

Mk places this story after the supper, on the road to Gethsemane (Mk 14:27–31). In Lk they are still in the upper room, and only Lk makes mention of Peter's restoration and ultimate leadership.

A time of crisis (Lk only)

22:35. *Purse or haversack.* This refers to the mission of the seventy-two (10:1–16).

38. *There are two swords here now.* The disciples took the words of Jesus literally, and he closed the conversation without explanation.

LUKE'S VERSION OF THE SUPPER

Scholars do not agree as to what Lk wrote originally about the supper because the mention of two cups, v. 17 and v. 20, has been a problem, and some early manuscripts omit vv. 19b–20. The New English Bible and the Revised Standard Version both follow the shorter form of the text, but the translators of the Jerusalem Bible have retained the longer version in the conviction that Lk had good reasons for his arrangement which the commentary tries to make plain. Lk's account of the supper differs considerably from that of Mk and he may have used a source which has never come to light.

The Mount of Olives (Mk 14:32–42)

Lk does not mention the name of the place, Gethsemane, and if he was using Mk's account, he shortened
it. Many early manuscripts omit vv. 43–44.

22:42. *Father, if you are willing* . . . The clause 'your will be
done' is not included in Lk's version of the Lord's
prayer (Lk 11:2–4; Mt 5:9–13). But here the supreme
example of its use is given.
Take this cup from me. The cup was the Old Testament
symbol for suffering. It is used in the same sense in
Mk's story of the sons of Zebedee (Mk 10:35–40),
and at the supper (v. 22).

The arrest (Mk 14:43–52; Mt 26:47–56; Jn 18:3–11)

In Mk and Mt Jesus was seized immediately after
Judas's greeting, the sword episode followed, and
then Jesus spoke to those who had come to arrest him.
But Lk like Jn puts the speech of Jesus before the
actual arrest, thus making clear that Jesus had full
control over what took place.

50. *His right ear.* This detail is given by Lk and Jn only.

51. *He healed him.* Lk only.

52. *Jesus spoke to the chief priests.* The authorities had
come in person to see that the arrest was made. In Mk
and Mt they sent armed men.

Peter's denials

In Lk the denial comes before the trial before the Sanhedrin (the council of the Jews—Intro B), which took
place in the early morning. In Mk and Mt there was a
hearing in the middle of the night, and another in the
early morning to confirm the earlier proceedings,
Peter's denial coming after the first hearing.

54. *They took him to the high priest's house.* Caiaphas (Mt

26:57; Jn 18:13), mentioned only by Lk at the beginning of John the Baptist's ministry (3:2).

22:61. *The Lord turned and looked at Peter* (Lk only). Peter became the leader of the apostles and it would be natural for loyal supporters to allow the story of his denials to be forgotten. This never happened because his restoration illustrated the measure of the Lord's forgiveness, and the measure of his power to work through a humble and penitent disciple.

Jesus before the Sanhedrin

66. *A meeting of the elders of the people.* The Sanhedrin met in full conclave.

67. *If you are the Christ, tell us.* According to Lk this was the single point at issue. There is no mention of false witnesses and Jesus having said that he could destroy the Temple and build it up in three days (Mk 14:57–58; Mt 26:60–61).

69. *From now on, the Son of Man will be seated at the right hand . . .* The glory and reign of Christ begin from his condemnation and suffering, an idea very prominent in Jn.

70. *You are the Son of God then?* The title was the equivalent of Son of David, the common Messianic title (5:24). Jesus did not deny it any more than he had at Jericho when he was hailed by the blind man (18:35–43).
It is you who say that I am. The description would have to serve. It was too late now for his questioners to grasp what even the disciples could not understand.

Jesus before Pilate

23   It was only the Roman Governor who had the authority to order the death penalty. The members of the Sanhedrin were no doubt genuinely afraid that Jesus would head a political movement which would result

in ruthless suppression by the Romans (Jn 11:47–51),
but they were also profoundly jealous of the authority
with which he spoke and acted, forgiving sins and
making light of the oral law (5:16–6:11).

23:2. *We found this man inciting our people to revolt* . . . The
three points were all political, the most important
being placed last.

3. *Are you the king of the Jews?* The emphasis should
probably be placed on the second word. There was
nothing in the appearance of Jesus to suggest that he
was aiming at worldly power. Jesus answered Pilate
as he had answered the members of the Sanhedrin and
for the same reason (22:70).

4. *I find no case against this man.* One of the purposes of
Luke–Acts was to show in what sense Jesus was king,
and that his claim had nothing to do with politics, and
all the gospels agree about Pilate's opinion (Mk 15:10).

7. *He passed him over to Herod* (9:7–9; 13:31–32). It was
a clever move on Pilate's part because Herod belonged
to the country and would be able to assess the situation better than he could, as a foreigner.

Jesus before Herod (Lk only)

Lk may have got this story through a member of the
Herod family at Antioch (8:3).

11. *He put a rich cloak on him.* In the other gospels it was
the Roman soldiers who mocked Jesus as a bogus
king, crowning him with thorns (Mk 15:16–20; Mt
27:27–31; Jn 19:2–3).

14–15. *I have . . . found no case against the man . . . Nor has
Herod.* Neither the Roman nor the Jewish political
authority thought there was a case against Jesus, and
that was enough to establish his innocence. The full
guilt for the final sentence lay with the Jewish leaders.

23:18. *Away with him! Give us Barabbas!* (Mk 15:8–9; Mt 27:15; Jn 18:39). 'At festival time it was the governor's practice to release a prisoner for the people, anyone they chose.'

22. *For the third time he spoke to them.* Pilate's conviction of the innocence of Jesus is underlined, and at the same time his own appalling weakness.

24. *Pilate then gave his verdict.* He passed the death sentence. Lk makes no mention of the scourging which always preceded Roman executions, and which the other three gospels record (Mk 15:15; Mt 27:26; Jn 19:1). There is only Pilate's suggestion that Jesus should be flogged and then released, v. 16 and v. 22.

The way to Calvary

In the Latin Bible that was used in western Europe up to the time of the Reformation, the Aramaic 'Golgotha', 'the place of a skull' (Mk 15:22) was translated 'Calvariae locus' and so our word 'calvary' came into use.

26. *Simon from Cyrene.* Cyrene was a North African province, the modern Cyrenaica. Simon's sons, Alexander and Rufus, became prominent in the Church at Rome (Mk 15:21–22).

They . . . made him shoulder the cross. It was usual practice to enforce the help of an able-bodied bystander. Because ancient pictures show the whole cross being carried, it is generally taken for granted that that was the procedure. In fact the weight of the whole cross would have been beyond any man's strength, and it was the cross-beam only that the victim had to carry.

27–31. Lk only.

29. *The days will surely come.* Another prediction of the destruction of Jerusalem (13:35; 19:43–44; 20:16; 21:6).

23:31. *If men use the green wood like this* . . . If green wood is burnt that is not meant for burning (allusion to Christ's condemnation), what is to happen to the dry wood (the truly guilty)?

The crucifixion (Mk 15:22–41; Mt 27:32–56)

Comparison with Mk shows how Lk has softened the harshness of calvary. The hostility of the crowds is not strongly emphasised and the despairing cry (Mk 15:34) has been omitted. On the other hand material has been included which is unique to this gospel, the words of Jesus v. 34 and v. 46, and the story of the good thief, vv. 39–43.

34. *Father, forgive them.* This is the climax of the teaching on forgiveness which is such an important element in this gospel. The Roman soldiers to whom the words seem to refer, were obliged to carry out orders and not responsible for what they did.

They cast lots to share out his clothing. This was the custom and some compensation for a prolonged and unpleasant task.

The crucified Christ is mocked

35. *Let him save himself if he is the Christ of God.* This is what the devil had suggested in the wilderness but Christ chose to accept human limitations (4:4) (Mt 26:53).

36. *The soldiers approached to offer him vinegar* (Mk 15:23; Mt 27:34). Wine mixed with myrrh was a drug provided by compassionate women of Jerusalem to help men undergoing crucifixion and Jesus refused it.

38. *Above him there was an inscription.* A placard was always put over the head of the crucified as a warning to passers-by.

This is the King of the Jews. Jesus reigns from the cross.

'And when I am lifted up from the earth,
I shall draw all men to myself' (Jn 12:32)

The good thief

There is a link here with Mk 15:32. 'Even those who were crucified with him taunted him.'

23:40. *Have you no fear of God at all?* The sharp contrast between the hard character and the one capable of response to the divine mercy, so characteristic of this gospel, finds a place even in the story of the Passion.

43. *Today you will be with me in Paradise.* The word 'paradise' meaning 'park' or 'garden' is used in the LXX (the Greek version of the Old Testament) for the garden of Eden (Genesis chs. 2–3). Adam and Eve were expelled from the garden and now Christ makes re-entry possible.

The death of Jesus

44. *About the sixth hour.* The Jews reckoned from sunrise so the darkness lasted from about twelve noon until three in the afternoon. It was the third hour (nine in the morning) that they crucified him (Mk 15:25)
With the sun eclipsed, a darkness came. Jesus had said that signs in the sun and moon would point to the inauguration of the kingdom (21:25) (Mk 15:33; 27:45).

45. *The veil of the Temple was torn right down the middle.* The destruction of the Temple had begun. The veil was the curtain which separated the Holy Place from the Holy of Holies, an empty room into which no one might go except the high priest on the Day of Atonement, the great fast day. The Temple was superseded by Christ who has opened the way to God for all men.

46. *Father, into your hands I commit my spirit.* The words are from Psalm 31:5. Mk 15:37, 'Jesus gave a loud cry.'

After the death

47. *The centurion . . . gave praise to God.* He was in charge of the soldiers who had carried out the execution. It was he, a gentile, who was first to recognise that Christ was guiltless.

23:48. *All the people . . . went home beating their breasts.* Whatever part they had played in shouting for the crucifixion of Jesus, they were sorry now.

49. *The women.* For their names see Mk 15:40–41.

The burial (Mk 15:42–47)

50. *A member of the council arrived . . . named Joseph.* Joseph of Arimathea was a member of the Sanhedrin and had therefore seen the development of the plot against Jesus. He is mentioned in all four gospels.

51. *He lived in hope of seeing the kingdom of God.* Like Simeon (2:25–32).

52. *This man went to Pilate and asked for the body of Jesus.* The authorities were naturally careful to ensure that death had actually taken place (Mk 15:44–45).

53. *A tomb which was hewn in stone.* Tombs of the same kind can still be seen in Palestine. They are small chambers hewn out of the rock with a narrow ledge down one side for the body.

54. *It was Preparation Day.* The sabbath began at sunset, about six o'clock, and as Jesus had died at about three, there was very little time to do all that was necessary before all work had to stop.

55. *The women . . . took note of the tomb.* They had witnessed everything and knew for certain where Jesus was buried.

VII. AFTER THE RESURRECTION

The empty tomb; the angel's message

24:1. *The body of the Lord Jesus was not there.* It is a very plain statement of fact.

24:4. *Two men in brilliant clothes* (Mk 16:5). 'A young man in a white robe.'

6. *He is not here; he has risen* (Mk 16:6).
Remember what he told you when he was still in Galilee. In Lk all the post-resurrection events take place in Jerusalem, the centre from which the world-wide mission expanded. This accounts for his difference from Mk 16:7 where it is the declared intention of Jesus, after the resurrection, to go before the disciples into Galilee.

The apostles refuse to believe the women

10. Mary of Magdala and Joanna (8:2) Mary the mother of James (Mk 15:40).

Peter at the tomb

12. The incident is recounted Jn 20:3–10 and Lk and Jn may well have drawn on a common source. In Lk the emphasis is on the amazement of Peter whereas in Jn the stress is on the belief and understanding of 'the other disciple'.

The road to Emmaus (Lk only)

13. *That very same day.* It is still the first day of the week.

16. *Something prevented them from recognising him.* In the appearances described by Lk and Jn the disciples do not at first recognise the Lord, but need a word or a sign (24:31–32). This is because the risen body, though the same body that died on the cross, is in a new condition. The outward appearance is changed and it is exempt from the usual physical laws.

18. *Cleopas* (Jn 19:25).

19. *What things?* Jesus led them to the right conclusion by means of his question, as during his ministry (9:18–20).
All about Jesus of Nazareth. Note the progression in

their conception of him; teacher, prophet, Messiah, and a dawning hope of his resurrection.

24:24. *Some of our friends.* Perhaps the visit made by Peter and John (Jn 20:3–10).

25. *You foolish men!* (18:31–34).

27. *Starting from Moses.* i.e. The first five books of the Old Testament, often called the Pentateuch, the most important part of the Scriptures to the Jews (16:29). Christ showed the disciples how God had from the beginning acted through events for the salvation of His people, and how his own coming was in keeping with all that had happened in the past.

30–31. *He took the bread . . . and their eyes were opened.* It was the action of the Eucharist (22:19), the sign by which he made himself known (v. 16).

34. *The Lord has risen and appeared to Simon.* The only story of an appearance to Peter is to be found in Jn 21:1–19, but St Paul supports the tradition that he was the first of the apostles to see the risen Christ (I Corinthians 15:5, Cephas being Peter's Aramaic name).

Jesus appears to the apostles (Jn 20:19–23)

Many Greeks believed in the immortality of the soul but the idea of the resurrection of the body was regarded as plainly absurd. In this passage Lk underlines the physical reality of Christ's risen body. His hands and feet bore the marks of the nails, he invited the disciples to touch him, and he ate before them. In considering this matter it is important to bear in mind the fact that the personality requires a body through which to express itself and by which to communicate with others. For light on this subject see I Corinthians 15:35–55.

Last instructions to the apostles (Mt 28:16–20)

44. *Then he told them.* It is still the first day of the week.

24:45. *He opened their minds to understand the scriptures* (v. 27). The Gospel is rooted in the teaching of the Old Testament, and so the Old Testament sheds light on the New.

47. *In his name.* For the tremendous implications of this phrase, 10:16–17.

48. *You are witnesses to this.* The apostles are witnesses to the fact of the resurrection, the basic doctrine of Christianity upon which everything else depends.

49. *What the Father has promised.* The gift of the Holy Spirit, 'the power from on high', bestowed at Pentecost (Acts 2:6–11) and foretold by the prophet Joel 3:1–5.

The Ascension (Acts 1:6–11)

50. *Bethany.* On the Mount of Olives; the village where Mary and Martha lived.
He withdrew from them and was carried up into heaven. The withdrawal of Jesus from the limits of time and space is expressed in picture language. He was never again visibly present to his disciples but they came to know that he was actually present with them all, no matter how great their number or how widely they were separated. He was with the Father.
They worshipped him. As good Jews the apostles knew the first commandment, 'You shall have no gods except me' (Exodus 20:3). They accepted their experience without thinking it out, full of joy and praising God. It was about twenty years later in the letters of St Paul that we have evidence of Christians thinking more clearly in terms of the Father, the Son, and the Holy Spirit.

53. *They were continually in the Temple.* Lk's gospel ends where it began, in the Temple: its last word is of joy and praise.